Greed in America:

The Numbers Don't Lie

By John Baker

2012 Edition

PREFACE

The unequal distribution of wealth in the United States is a subject that has become of vital concern to many Americans. While the average worker faces stagnant or declining real wages, the fortunes of the super-rich continue to soar. As such, there seems to be no correlation between the plight of the economy as a whole and the financial position of the wealthiest members of our society: the financial elite continue to flourish while the rest of the nation struggles. Because of this apparent injustice, many people are beginning to question the ethics of a select few members of our society possessing astronomical fortunes while the masses find themselves in a tenuous financial position.

Greed in America: the Numbers Don't Lie is intended to aid the people in their analysis of economic inequality by putting into perspective the true significance and magnitude of great wealth in the United States. This is accomplished by means of translating into concrete and easily understood terms the practically incomprehensible abstraction of "billions" of dollars of wealth.

The statistics and calculations presented in this book are absolute and indisputable facts. The net worth of each person examined in this book was obtained not from the so-called "liberal media", but rather from that paragon of unapologetic capitalism, *Forbes*. At any point in time in which you question the validity of any of the startling computations in this book, you can, if you wish, grab a calculator and a copy of *Forbes* magazine's 400 Richest Americans and perform the simple yet powerful calculations for yourself.

This book is divided into two sections: Part A: *Just the Facts, Ma'am* and Part B: *That's Entertainment!*

Part A: *Just the Facts, Ma'am* is primarily comprised of statistics and simple mathematical calculations. The data used in this section is factual. There is the occasional ironic or sarcastic comment on my part which is intended to add zest to the discussion.

Part B: *That's Entertainment!* is a type of literary satire which exposes the inherent injustice of extreme economic inequality and the callousness of those lucky few who are members of America's financial elite. The purpose of this section of the book is to reflect the spirit and essence of the entrenched mindset of the super-rich and the frustration and exasperation of those members of our society who are struggling simply to get by.

PART A:

JUST THE FACTS, MA'AM

"The love of money is the root of all evil."

-The Holy Bible, The First Epistle

of Paul the Apostle to Timothy

6:10

"Greed is good."

-John Stossel

TIME IS MONEY,

ESPECIALLY IF YOU'RE A BILLIONAIRE

Let us begin our examination of the American billionaire with the ubiquitous Oprah Winfrey. Ms. Winfrey's rise to the ranks of billionaire has been nothing short of phenomenal. In less than fifty-seven short years, she has managed to earn a staggering $2.7 BILLION. Hypothetically, if the wise and benevolent O had begun to earn her fortune the moment she was born, she would have needed to average the following amounts of money per time period in order to reach $2.7 BILLION by her fifty-seventh birthday:

$47.4 MILLION PER YEAR

$3.95 MILLION PER MONTH

$131,667 PER DAY

$5,486 PER HOUR

$91.44 PER MINUTE

At $131,667 per day, this means that by the 8th DAY of her life, she would have already reached the lofty sum of

$1 MILLION

By the 16th day of her existence, little baby Oprah would have already become a

MULTIMILLIONAIRE

If Oprah's massive wealth of $2.7 BILLION were averaged out evenly over her lifetime, the all-powerful O's net worth would have needed to accumulate as follows:

1 (Year old) / $47.4 MILLION (Net Worth)

2 / $94.8 MILLION

3 / $142.2 MILLION

4 / $189.6 MILLION

5 / $237 MILLION

6 / $284.4 MILLION

7 / $331.8 MILLION

8 / $379.2 MILLION

9 / $426.6 MILLION

10 / $474 MILLION

At the rate of $47.4 MILLION per year, she would have become a

BILLIONAIRE

by the time she reached the ripe old age of

TWENTY-ONE

AVERAGE JOAN VS. OPRAH

As a comparison to the great and powerful O, and to show how unimaginably massive $2.7 BILLION is, if a fifty-seven-year-old person with a net worth of $300,000 had begun to earn her net worth the moment she was born, she would have needed to average the following sums of money per time period in order to reach a substantial net worth of $300,000 by the time she reached fifty-seven years of age. Oprah's rise in wealth is shown below Average Joan's as a comparison:

AVERAGE JOAN

Per Year: $5,263

Per Month: $438.6

Per Day: $14.62

Per Hour: $0.61 (61 Cents)

Per Minute: $0.0102 (1.02 Cents)

OPRAH

Per Year: $47,400,000

Per Month: $3,950,000

Per Day: $131,667

Per Hour: $5,486

Per Minute: $91.44

Over the first ten years of her life, Average Joan's net worth relative to Oprah's would have grown as follows:

AVERAGE JOAN

1 Year Old / $5,263 (Accumulated Wealth)

2 Years Old / $10,526 (Accumulated Wealth)

3 Years Old / $15,789 (Accumulated Wealth)

4 Years Old / $21,052 (Accumulated Wealth)

5 Years Old / $26,315 (Accumulated Wealth)

6 Years Old / $31,578 (Accumulated Wealth)

7 Years Old / $36,841 (Accumulated Wealth)

8 Years Old / $42,104 (Accumulated Wealth)

9 Years Old / $47,367 (Accumulated Wealth)

10 Years Old / $52,630 (Accumulated Wealth)

1 (Year Old) / <u>$47,400,000</u> (Accumulated Wealth)

2 Years Old / <u>$94,800,000</u> (Accumulated Wealth)

3 Years Old / <u>$142,200,000</u> (Accumulated Wealth)

4 Years Old / <u>$189,600,000</u> (Accumulated Wealth)

5 Years Old / <u>$237,000,000</u> (Accumulated Wealth)

6 Years Old / <u>284,400,000</u> (Accumulated Wealth)

7 Years Old / <u>331,800,000</u> (Accumulated Wealth)

8 Years Old / <u>379,200,000</u> (Accumulated Wealth)

9 Years Old / <u>426,600,000 (</u>Accumulated Wealth)

10 Years Old / <u>474,000,000</u> (Accumulated Wealth)

At this rate, it would take Average Joan TWENTY-FIVE YEARS to earn the amount of money that Oprah would have earned the FIRST DAY OF HER LIFE ($131,667).

A JOURNEY OF 2.2 MILLION ACRES BEGINS

WITH A SINGLE *CROOKED* STEP

Have you ever wondered why the price of land is so high? Perhaps it's because America's billionaires have gobbled up so much of it. Presented below is a list of America's greediest landowners and the amount of land they have managed to purchase with their practically illimitable wealth:

Landed Aristocrat's Name / Net Worth / Acres Owned

John Malone / $3 Billion / 2.2 **MILLION** ACRES OWNED

Ted Turner / $1.9 Billion / 2.1 **MILLION** ACRES OWNED

Red Emmerson / $2.5 Billion / 1.72 **MILLION** ACRES OWNED

Brad Kelley / $1.5 Billion / 1.7 **MILLION** ACRES OWNED

Irving Family / $4 Billion / 1.2 **MILLION** ACRES OWNED

Singleton Family / Less than $1 Billion / 1.1 MILLION ACRES OWNED

Total Acres Collectively Owned: 10.02 MILLION ACRES

As you can see, John Malone from Liberty Media is the largest landowner in the United States. 2.2 MILLION ACRES, John Malone's total land holdings, equal

3,437.5 SQUARE MILES

This means that Mr. Malone possesses more land than is contained in the following states:

State / Total Land Area

Rhode Island / 1,545 Square Miles

Delaware / 2,489 Square Miles

John Malone's land holdings of 2.2 MILLION Acres are equal to

95.832 BILLION SQUARE FEET

If John Malone's total land holdings were all contained in one square-shaped property, it would have dimensions of 58.63 MILLES in length by 58.63 MILLES in width.

If Mr. Malone decided to drive from the exact center of his square-shaped property down his driveway at 50 mph, it would take him over

35 minutes

to reach the edge of his property.

If he drove from one end of his property to the other at 50 mph, it would take him over

1 hour and 10 minutes

to complete his arduous journey.

If he decided to drive around the entire perimeter of his massive property at **50 mph** to inspect the electrical fence designed to keep the riff raff out, his journey would last over

4 hours and 40 minutes.

The total number of acres owned by the top six landowners in the United States is

10.02 MILLION ACRES

OR

15,656.25 SQUARE MILES

This is larger than the total land area in each of the following states:

State / Total Land Area (Square Miles)

Rhode Island: <u>1,545</u> Square Miles

Delaware: <u>2,489</u> Square Miles

Connecticut: <u>5,543</u> Square Miles

New Jersey: <u>8,721</u> Square Miles

New Hampshire: <u>9,350</u> Square Miles

Vermont: <u>9,614</u> Square Miles

Massachusetts: <u>10,555</u> Square Miles

Hawaii: <u>10,931</u> Square Miles

Maryland: <u>12,407</u> Square Miles

Here are a few examples of some <u>COUNTRIES</u> with total land areas LESS than the six plutocrats above:

Belgium: <u>11,787</u> Square miles

Lebanon: <u>4,015</u> Square Miles

Israel: <u>8,522</u> Square Miles

Haiti: <u>10,714</u> Square Miles

Jamaica: <u>4,244</u> Square Miles

Albania: <u>11,100</u> Square Miles

Taiwan: <u>13,892</u> Square Miles

Puerto Rico: <u>3,515</u> Square Miles

One billion dollars in one dollar bills weighs approximately

2.2 *MILLION* POUNDS

OR

1,102 *TONS*

This is the equivalent to approximately <u>469</u> Ford F-150 pickup trucks.

If Bill Gates hired some neighborhood kid to move one billion dollars from one end of his mansion to another, and this kid - who incidentally would probably be paid minimum wage for this task - could move 50 pounds of one dollar bills at a time, it would take him 44,000 trips. If he could make one trip per minute, it would take this kid 733 hours or 30 straight days to complete his task if he worked 24 hours per day. If he put in eight-hour days, it would take him over 91 days. If he were given the job of moving Bill Gate's net worth of $59 billion in one dollar bills, it would take him 2,596,000 trips or 43,247 hours or 5,405 days or 14.8 years if he worked eight hours per day, 365 days per year.

If this same kid were asked to move a general practitioner's yearly salary of say $200,000, it would only take him 9 trips, or 9 minutes to complete his task.

And you thought doctors made a lot of money.

The moon's average distance from the earth is 238,857 miles. If Oprah's net worth of $2.7 BILLION in one dollar bills were placed end to end, it would stretch approximately

261,144 MILES

OR

22,287 MILES

BEYOND THE MOON

At a staggering $17.5 BILLION, Mark "Baby Facebook" Zuckerberg's net worth in one dollar bills placed end to end would stretch

1,692,600 MILES

OVER 7 TIMES THE DISTANCE OF THE EARTH FROM THE MOON.

Bill Gates, the richest person in the United States, has a net worth of $59 BILLION. If this staggering sum of money in one dollar bills were placed end to end, it would stretch approximately

5,706,480 MILES

or

OVER *23 TIMES*

THE DISTANCE OF THE EARTH

FROM THE MOON.

The total net worth of the 400 richest people in the United States of America is an unfathomable $1,500,000,000,000. If their $1.5 TRILLION fortune in one dollar bills were placed end to end, it would stretch

145,080,000 MILES

or

OVER 52 MILLION MILES

PAST THE SUN!

By comparison, if a wheat farmer's net worth of $200,000 in one dollar bills were placed end to end, it would only stretch

19.4 MILES

OR

238,838 MILES SHY

OF REACHING THE MOON

WHEELBARROWS AND WHEELBARROWS

FULL OF MONEY

If Michael Bloomberg needed to transport his $19.5 BILLION fortune from one bank to another, this amount of money in one dollar bills would fill the following number of six-cubic-feet wheelbarrows:

116,705 WHEELBARROWS

By comparison, $50,000 in one dollar bills would fill only:

1/3 of a wheelbarrow

Come to think of it, for this amount of money, you wouldn't even need a wheelbarrow but could use a couple of lunch pails instead.

BILLION DOLLAR BABY

By now, everybody on the planet is familiar with Facebook's T-shirt-clad creator, Mark Zuckerberg. His ascent into the upper echelons of the U.S. plutocracy has been meteoric. In the click of a mouse, he has gone from a nerdy student at Harvard University to a nerdy multi-billionaire. At last count, his ever skyrocketing net worth is estimated to be $17.5 BILLION. Hypothetically, if his wealth were evenly distributed throughout his life, he would have needed to accumulate the following sums of money within the *first hour after his birth* to reach $17.5 BILLION by the age of twenty-seven:

15 Minutes Old : $18,497 (Accumulated Wealth)

30 Minutes Old : $36,994 (Accumulated Wealth)

45 Minutes Old : $55,491 (Accumulated Wealth)

60 Minutes Old : $73,989 (Accumulated Wealth)

Here is the amount of money he needed to earn the *first ten minutes of his life* in order to reach $17.5 BILLION by the age of 27:

1 Minute Old : $1,233 (Accumulated Wealth)

2 Minutes Old : $2,466 (Accumulated Wealth)

3 Minutes Old : $3,699 (Accumulated Wealth)

4 Minutes Old : $4,932 (Accumulated Wealth)

5 Minutes Old : $6,165 (Accumulated Wealth)

6 Minutes Old : $7,398 (Accumulated Wealth)

7 Minutes Old : $8,631 (Accumulated Wealth)

8 Minutes Old : $9,864 (Accumulated Wealth)

9 Minutes Old: $11,097 (Accumulated Wealth)

10 Minutes Old : $12,330 (Accumulated Wealth)

And in order to accumulate $17.5 BILLION in 27 short years, he would have needed to average over $20.55 *PER SECOND* (24 hours per day, 365 days per year for 27 years) *from the moment he was born.*

1 (Second Old)   : $20.55 (Accumulated Wealth)

2 (Seconds Old) : $41.10 (Accumulated Wealth)

3 (Seconds Old) : $61.65 (Accumulated Wealth)

4 Seconds Old : $82.20 (Accumulated Wealth)

5 Seconds Old : $102.75 (Accumulated Wealth)

6 Seconds Old : 123.30 (Accumulated Wealth)

7 Seconds Old : $143.85 (Accumulated Wealth)

8 Seconds Old : $164.40 (Accumulated Wealth)

9 Seconds Old : $184.95 (Accumulated Wealth)

10 Seconds Old: $205.50 (Accumulated

Wealth)

A Rolls-Royce is one of those possessions that is emblematic of wealth. Few people would even dare to dream of possessing such and extravagance. Oprah Winfrey is one of the select few who could dare to purchase one of these exceedingly expensive vehicles without even batting an eye. In fact, if she decided to use her massive wealth of $2.7 billion to buy a few Rolls-Royces, she could purchase

7,105 $380,000 Rolls-Royce Phantoms

Since Rolls Royce only produces about 500 Phantoms per year, Oprah could hypothetically buy every single Phantom produced in the world for the next fourteen years.

As some of you may be aware, one's jobsite can be a very dangerous place. In fact, every year thousands of people are killed while at work. The following shows the number of workers who were KILLED on the job in 2008 in specific industries:

AGRICULTURE: 623

MINING: 172

CONSTRUCTION: 932

TRANSPORTATION AND WAREHOUSING: 691

BILLIONAIRES: 0

It is a tremendous relief to know that not a single billionaire was killed on the job in 2008. In all fairness, however, it has been rumored that Bill Gates may have pulled a muscle while attempting to lift a humungous duffle bag crammed with $100 bills.

FOR THE MASSES

The number of years it would take an elementary school teacher who earns $50,000 per year to accumulate $1 BILLION:

20,000 YEARS

This means that if the school teacher had started to earn $50,000 per year in the year 17,990 B.C., she would not have reached $1 BILLION until the year 2010 A.D.

Here is our exhausted teacher's seemingly unending journey to $1 BILLION:

Year

17,990 B.C.

Teacher's Wealth

$0

Year

16,666 B.C.

This Year in History

Rupert Murdock is born. His mother successfully conceals

his red eyes, long tail, and mysterious grouping of numbers

on his head.

Year

14,526 B.C.

This Year in History

Klug, the richest caveman in the world,

owns 37 caves, 52 cave women, and

23,742 wooden clubs.

Year

13,990 B.C.

Years of Labor

4,000

Teacher's Accumulated Net Worth

$200 Million

Year

11,039 B.C.

This Year in History

The game "Rock" is invented; paper and scissors are added several thousand years later.

Year

9,990 B.C.

Years of Labor

8,000

Teacher's Accumulated Net Worth

$400 Million

Year

7,612 B.C.

This Year in History

Greedy Mr. Slate makes 315 times that which
rock quarry employee Fred Flintstone earns.

Year

5,990 B.C.

Years of Labor

12,000

Teacher's Accumulated Net Worth

$600 Million

Year

1,990 B.C.

Years of Labor

16,000

Teacher's Accumulated Net Worth

$800 Million

Year

1,878 B.C.

This Year in History

For the first time in the history of "mankind", a war for
profit is not taking place somewhere in the world. This
unfortunate occurrence lasts for approximately 42 ½
minutes before things return to normal.

Year

1492

This Year in History

Christopher Columbus enslaves countless indigenous
people in the Caribbean in pursuit of shiny gold. Several
hundred years later, he is honored for his efforts by the
United States of America with a holiday in his name.

Year

1599

This Year in History

Shakespeare's dog, Horatio, secretly writes the play,
"Hamlet". Shakespeare steals manuscript and enjoys fame
and fortune; Horatio ends up homeless and living in a ditch
in Blackmoor.

Year

1776

This Year in History

The Declaration of Independence is penned by slave owners.

Year

2010

Years of Labor

20,000

Teacher's Accumulated Net Worth

$1 Billion

WE'RE THE KINGS OF THE WORLD!

The combined net worth of the Forbes 400 Gang, a.k.a. *La Cosa Nostra*, is

$1.5 TRILLION

Or

2.4% of the TOTAL WEALTH

of the United States of America

Even though they represent only

.00013% or just 1/13 MILLIONTH of
the population

This seems to be an equitable distribution of wealth, don't you think?

As one billionaire said to another, "Works for me."

THE FRESH KING OF BEVERLY HILLS

The Beverly House in Beverly Hills, California, the former residence of publishing magnate William Randolph Hearst, has an estimated worth of $165 million. This staggering sum of money is beyond the means of most families in America not to mention most kings and sultans around the world. For Bill Gates, however, this would be the perfect starter home. As such, if he ever decided to move from overcast Seattle to the sun-bathed estates of Beverly Hills, he could buy the Hearst mansion and still have

$58.835 BILLION of his $59 BILLION net worth left.

With a net worth of $59 billion, Mr. Gates would not have to settle for only one such estate, but could purchase

THREE HUNDRED AND FIFTY-SEVEN $165 MILLION ESTATES

Heck, with his kind of money, maybe he could buy every estate in Beverly Hills.

The average American individual salary (2008)

$45,563

The number of average salaries it takes to equal Oprah Winfrey's net worth:

59,258

The number of average American individual salaries it takes to equal the combined net worth of the Forbes 400 Gang:

32,921,000

That's more than 32 *MILLION* salaries.

This is just slightly less than the *entire*

population of Canada.

If Christy Walton (one of the co-owners of the Walmart corporation), donated just half of her $24.5 BILLION fortune to the poor and needy, she would still be left with $12.25 BILLION on which to subsist.

This donated sum of $12.25 BILLION could then be given in $100,000 increments to

125,000 POOR AND DESPERATE FAMILIES

This is more than the population of the entire city of Canton, Ohio (73,000)

This means that the equivalent of every man, woman and child in Canton, Ohio plus 52,000 people in surrounding areas would be $100,000 richer if only Christy would simply release her iron grip on some of her precious billions

HOW LOW CAN YOU GO?

The U.S. Poverty Threshold by Family Size for 2008

1 Person: $10,991

2 People: $14,051

3 People: $17,163

4 People: $22,025

Based on these statistics, if you make more than these minimums, you are technically not living in poverty. As an example, a person who lives alone and earns $10,992 per year is technically not living in poverty.

By comparison, Oprah, who is just one person, surpassed the minimum earning requirement of $10,991 in only 21 minutes or "work" in 2007-2008. As such, if she had started work on January 2, 2007 at 9:00 A.M., she would have "earned" more than the poverty threshold level of $10,991 by 9:21 A.M. of the *same day*.

In the third quarter of 2009, the number of foreclosure filings in the United States hit a record high of 937,840. This means that *one in every 136 homes* in the United States was in foreclosure.

If the Forbes 400 Gang had simply relaxed their death grip on only ONE TENTH of their massive collective net worth of $1.5 TRILLION, they could have given to *each of the 937,840 families* in foreclosure a check for over $160,000.

How many people could have kept their homes if our greedy billionaires had just had a modicum of compassion?

This amount of money donated to desperate homeowners would have resulted in a change of net worth for our bodacious billionaires as follows:

Oprah

Hypothetical Donation

$270 million

Net Worth Remaining

$2.43 BILLION

Michael Bloomberg

Hypothetical Donation

$1.95 BILLION

Net worth Remaining

$17.55 BILLION

Donald Trump

Hypothetical Donation

$290 million

Net Worth Remaining

$2.61 BILLION

Warren Buffett

Hypothetical Donation

$3.9 billion

Net Worth Remaining

$35.1 BILLION

Bill Gates

Hypothetical Donation

$5.9 billion

Net Worth Remaining

$53.1 BILLION

If Bill Gates suddenly lost *99%* of his net worth, he would still be left with a staggering

$590 MILLION

If the Forbes 400 Richest People in the United States suddenly lost *99%* of their collective net worth, they would still be left with

$15 BILLION

If the Forbes 400 Richest People in the United States suddenly lost *99.9%* of their collective fortune, they'd still be left with a massive

$1.5 BILLION

These guys can't lose, can they?

"Money is like muck: not good except it be spread."

-Francis Bacon

"You're fired!"

-Donald Trump

I'M NOT A SMART MAN,

BUT I KNOW WHAT GREED IS

If one thinks deeply about the issue, it seems to be apparent that the accumulation of excess wealth can only be justified by two factors:

1. Greater than average intelligence and/or creativity.

2. Working harder and/or longer than the average person.

If this is understood to be true, then this would have to mean that if a person earns only what he or she justly deserves through hard work or greater intelligence/creativity, then Oprah Winfrey, who "earned" $275 million in one year, as compared to the average worker's salary of $45,000, is more than

6,000 TIMES SMARTER

THAN THE AVERAGE AMERICAN

Or

WORKS 6,000 TIMES HARDER

THAN THE AVERAGE AMERICAN

Or some combination of these two factors.

With "earnings" of $275 million, she "earned" 916 Times More than a BRAIN SURGEON who earned $300,000 in that same year or 4,230 Times More than a COAL MINER who earned $65,000. In order to JUSTIFY this massive disparity in earnings, it would have to mean that she was 916 times smarter than a BRAIN SURGEON and worked 4,230 times harder than a COAL MINER that year. These relationships are presented below.

OPRAH'S INTELLIGENCE VS A BRAIN SURGEON

EARNINGS June 2007-June 2008

OPRAH: $275 MILLION

BRAIN SURGEON: $300,000

If income can be justified by intelligence, then

I = INTELLIGENCE

BRAIN SURGEON'S INTELLIGENCE

II

50

OPRAH'S INTELLIGENCE

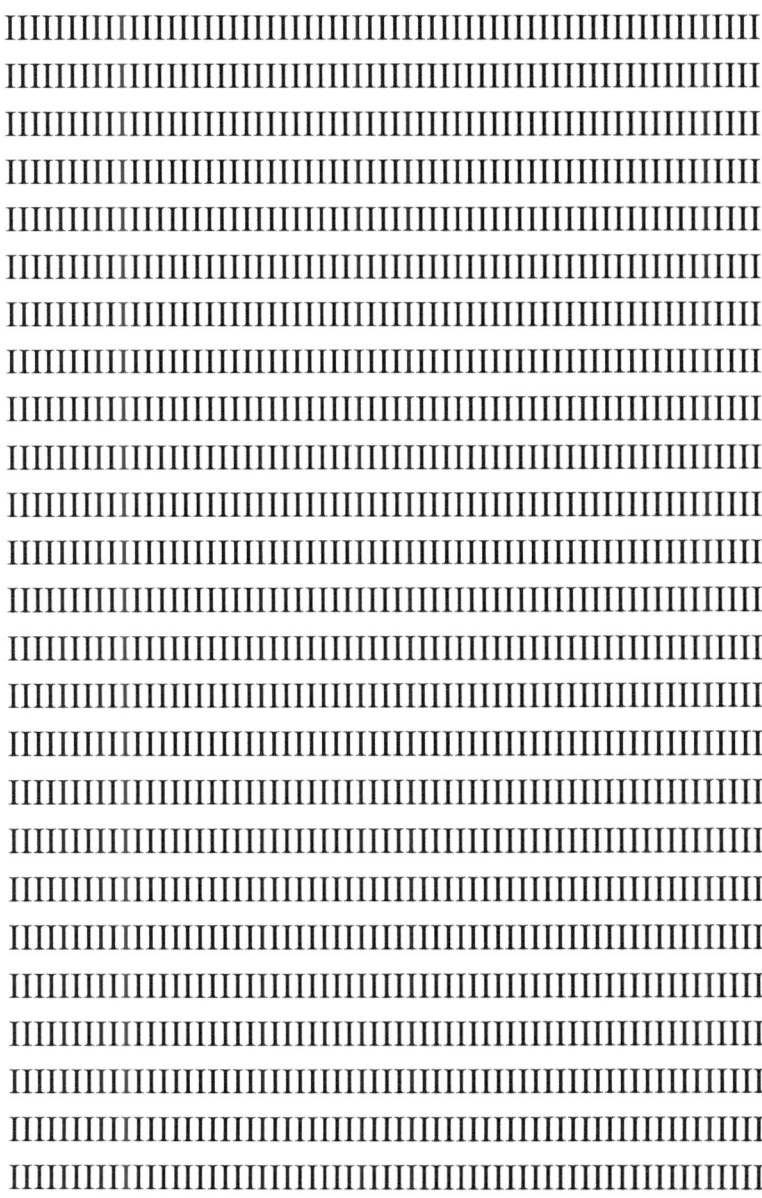

IIIIIIIIIIIIIIIIIIIIIIIIIIIIIIIIIIIIIIIIIIIIIIIIIIIIIIIIIIIIIIIIIII
IIIIIIIIIIIIIIIIIIIIIIIIIIIIIIIIIIIIIIIIIIIIIIIIIIIIIIIIIIIIIIIIIII
IIIIIIIIIIIIIIIIIIIIIIIIIIIIIIIIIIIIIIIIIIIIIIIIIIIIIIIIIIIIIIIIIII
IIIIIIIIIIIIIIIIIIIIIIIIIIIIIIIIIIIIIIIIIIIIIIIIIIIIIIIIIIIIIIIIIII
IIIIIIIIIIIIIIIIIIIIIIIIIIIIIIIIIIIIIIIIIIIIIIIIIIIIIIIIIIIIIIIIIII
III

OPRAH'S WORK EFFORT VS A COAL MINER

June 2007-June 2008 EARNINGS

OPRAH: $275 MILLION

COAL MINER: $65,000

If income can be justified by work effort, then

W = WORK EFFORT

COAL MINER'S WORK EFFORT

W

OPRAH'S WORK EFFORT

WWWWWWWWWWWWWWWWWWWWWWWW
WWWWWWWWWWWWWWWWWWWWWWWW
WWWWWWWWWWWWWWWWWWWWWWWW
WWWWWWWWWWWWWWWWWWWWWWWW
WWWWWWWWWWWWWWWWWWWWWWWW
WWWWWWWWWWWWWWWWWWWWWWWW
WWWWWWWWWWWWWWWWWWWWWWWW
WWWWWWWWWWWWWWWWWWWWWWWW
WWWWWWWWWWWWWWWWWWWWWWWW
WWWWWWWWWWWWWWWWWWWWWWWW
WWWWWWWWWWWWWWWWWWWWWWWW
WWWWWWWWWWWWWWWWWWWWWWWW
WWWWWWWWWWWWWWWWWWWWWWWW

WWWWWWWWWWWWWWWWWWWWWWWW
WWWWWWWWWWWWWWWWWWWWWWWW
WWWWWWWWWWWWWWWWWWWWWWWW
WWWWWWWWWWWWWWWWWWWWWWWW
WWWWWWWWWWWWWWWWWWWWWWWW
WWWWWWWWWWWWWWWWWWWWWWWW
WWWWWWWWWWWWWWWWWWWWWWWW
WWWWWWWWWWWWWWWWWWWWWWWW
WWWWWWWWWWWWWWWWWWWWWWWW
WWWWWWWWWWWWWWWWWWWWWWWW
WWWWWWWWWWWWWWWWWWWWWWWW
WWWWWWWWWWWWWWWWWWWWWWWW
WWWWWWWWWWWWWWWWWWWWWWWW
WWWWWWWWWWWWWWWWWWWWWWWW
WWWWWWWWWWWWWWWWWWWWWWWW
WWWWWWWWWWWWWWWWWWWWWWWW
WWWWWWWWWWWWWWWWWWWWWWWW
WWWWWWWWWWWWWWWWWWWWWWWW
WWWWWWWWWWWWWWWWWWWWWWWW
WWWWWWWWWWWWWWWWWWWWWWWW
WWWWWWWWWWWWWWWWWWWWWWWW
WWWWWWWWWWWWWWWWWWWWWWWW
WWWWWWWWWWWWWWWWWWWWWWWW
WWWWWWWWWWWWWWWWWWWWWWWW
WWWWWWWWWWWWWWWWWWWWWWWW
WWWWWWWWWWWWWWWWWWWWWWWW
WWWWWWWWWWWWWWWWWWWWWWWW
WWWWWWWWWWWWWWWWWWWWWWWW
WWWWWWWWWWWWWWWWWWWWWWWW
WWWWWWWWWWWWWWWWWWWWWWWW
WWWWWWWWWWWWWWWWWWWWWWWW

WWWWWWWWWWWWWWWWWWWWWWWWWWWWWW
WWWWWWWWWWWWWWWWWWWWWWWWWWWWWW
WWWWWWWWWWWWWWWWWWWWWWWWWWWWWW
WWWWWWWWWWWWWWWWWWWWWWWWWWWWWW
WWWWWWWWWWWWWWWWWWWWWWWWWWWWWW
WWWWWWWWWWWWWWWWWWWWWWWWWWWWWW
WWWWWWWWWWWWWWWWWWWWWWWWWWWWWW
WWWWWWWWWWWWWWWWWWWWWWWWWWWWWW
WWWWWWWWWWWWWWWWWWWWWWWWWWWWWW
WWWWWWWWWWWWWWWWWWWWWWWWWWWWWW
WWWWWWWWWWWWWWWWWWWWWWWWWWWWWW
WWWWWWWWWWWWWWWWWWWWWWWWWWWWWW
WWWWWWWWWWWWWWWWWWWWWWWWWWWWWW
WWWWWWWWWWWWWWWWWWWWWWWWWWWWWW
WWWWWWWWWWWWWWWWWWWWWWWWWWWWWW
WWWWWWWWWWWWWWWWWWWWWWWWWWWWWW
WWWWWWWWWWWWWWWWWWWWWWWWWWWWWW
WWWWWWWWWWWWWWWWWWWWWWWWWWWWWW
WWWWWWWWWWWWWWWWWWWWWWWWWWWWWW
WWWWWWWWWWWWWWWWWWWWWWWWWWWWWW
WWWWWWWWWWWWWWWWWWWWWWWWWWWWWW
WWWWWWWWWWWWWWWWWWWWWWWWWWWWWW
WWWWWWWWWWWWWWWWWWWWWWWWWWWWWW
WWWWWWWWWWWWWWWWWWWWWWWWWWWWWW
WWWWWWWWWWWWWWWWWWWWWWWWWWWWWW
WWWWWWWWWWWWWWWWWWWWWWWWWWWWWW
WWWWWWWWWWWWWWWWWWWWWWWWWWWWWW
WWWWWWWWWWWWWWWWWWWWWWWWWWWWWW
WWWWWWWWWWWWWWWWWWWWWWWWWWWWWW
WWWWWWWWWWWWWWWWWWWWWWWWWWWWWW
WWWWWWWWWWWWWWWWWWWWWWWWWWWWWW
WWWWWWWWWWWWWWWWWWWWWWWWWWWWWW
WWWWWWWWWWWWWWWWWWWWWWWWWWWWWW
WWWWWWWWWWWWWWWWWWWWWWWWWWWWWW

WWWWWWWWWWWWWWWWWWWWWWWW
WWWWWWWWWWWWWWWWWWWWWWWW
WWWWWWWWWWWWWWWWWWWWWWWW
WWWWWWWWWWWWWWWWWWWWWWWW
WWWWWWWWWWWWWWWWWWWWWWWW
WWWWWWWWWWWWWWWWWWWWWWWW
WWWWWWWWWWWWWWWWWWWWWWWW
WWWWWWWWWWWWWWWWWWWWWWWW
WWWWWWWWWWWWWWWWWWWWWWWW
WWWWWWWWWWWWWWWWWWWWWWWW
WWWWWWWWWWWWWWWWWWWWWWWW
WWWWWWWWWWWWWWWWWWWWWWWW
WWWWWWWWWWWWWWWWWWWWWWWW
WWWWWWWWWWWWWWWWWWWWWWWW
WWWWWWWWWWWWWWWWWWWWWWWW
WWWWWWWWWWWWWWWWWWWWWWWW
WWWWWWWWWWWWWWWWWWWWWWWW
WWWWWWWWWWWWWWWWWWWWWWWW
WWWWWWWWWWWWWWWWWWWWWWWW
WWWWWWWWWWWWWWWWWWWWWWWW
WWWWWWWWWWWWWWWWWWWWWWWW
WWWWWWWWWWWWWWWWWWWWWWWW
WWWWWWWWWWWWWWWWWWWWWWWW
WWWWWWWWWWWWWWWWWWWWWWWW
WWWWWWWWWWWWWWWWWWWWWWWW
WWWWWWWWWWWWWWWWWWWWWWWW
WWWWWWWWWWWWWWWWWWWWWWWW
WWWWWWWWWWWWWWWWWWWWWWWW
WWWWWWWWWWWWWWWWWWWWWWWW
WWWWWWWWWWWWWWWWWWWWWWWW

WWWWWWWWWWWWWWWWWWWWWWWW
WWWWWWWWWWWWWWWWWWWWWWWW
WWWWWWWWWWWWWWWWWWWWWWWW
WWWWWWWWWWWWWWWWWWWWWWWW
WWWWWWWWWWWWWWWWWWWWWWWW
WWWWWWWWWWWWWWWWWWWWWWWW
WWWWWWWWWWWWWWWWWWWWWWWW
WWWWWWWWWWWWWWWWWWWWWWWW
WWWWWWWWWWWWWWWWWWWWWWWW
WWWWWWWWWWWWWWWWWWWWWWWW
WWWWWWWWWWWWWWWWWWWWWWWW
WWWWWWWWWWWWWWWWWWWWWWWW
WWWWWWWWWWWWWWWWWWWWWWWW
WWWWWWWWWWWWWWWWWWWWWWWW
WWWWWWWWWWWWWWWWWWWWWWWW
WWWWWWWWWWWWWWWWWWWWWWWW
WWWWWWWWWWWWWWWWWWWWWWWW
WWWWWWWWWWWWWWWWWWWWWWWW
WWWWWWWWWWWWWWWWWWWWWWWW
WWWWWWWWWWWWWWWWWWWWWWWW
WWWWWWWWWWWWWWWWWWWWWWWW
WWWWWWWWWWWWWWWWWWWWWWWW
WWWWWWWWWWWWWWWWWWWWWWWW
WWWWWWWWWWWWWWWWWWWWWWWW
WWWWWWWWWWWWWWWWWWWWWWWW
WWWWWWWWWWWWWWWWWWWWWWWW
WWWWWWWWWWWWWWWWWWWWWWWW
WWWWWWWWWWWWWWWWWWWWWWWW
WWWWWWWWWWWWWWWWWWWWWWWW
WWWWWWWWWWWWWWWWWWWWWWWW

WWWWWWWWWWWWWWWWWWWWWW
WWWWWWWWWWWWWWWWWWWWWW
WWWWWWWWWWWWWWWWWWWWWW
WWWWWWWWWWWWWWWWWWWWWW
WWWWWWWWWWWWWWWWWWWWWW
WWWWWWWWWWWWWWWWWWWWWW
WWWWWWWWWWWWWWWWWWWWWW
WWWWWWWWWWWWWWWWWWWWWW
WWWWWWWWWWWWWWWWWWWWWW
WWWWWWWWWWWWWWWWWWWWWW
WWWWWWWWWWWWWWWWWWWWWW
WWWWWWWWWWWWWWWWWWWWWW
WWWWWWWWWWWWWWWWWWWWWW
WWWWWWWWWWWWWWWWWWWWWW
WWWWWWWWWWWWWWWWWWWWWW
WWWWWWWWWWWWWWWWWWWWWW
WWWWWWWWWWWWWWWWWWWWWW
WWWWWWWWWWWWWWWWWWWWWW
WWWWWWWWWWWWWWWWWWWWWW
WWWWWWWWWWWWWWWWWWWWWW
WWWWWWWWWWWWWWWWWWWWWW
WWWWWWWWWWWWWWWWWWWWWW
WWWWWWWWWWWWWWWWWWWWWW
WWWWWWWWWWWWWWWWWWWWWW
WWWWWWWWWWWWWWWWWWWWWW
WWWWWWWWWWWWWWWWWWWWWW
WWWWWWWWWWWWWWWWWWWWWW
WWWWWWWWWWWWWWWWWWWWWW
WWWWWWWWWWWWWWWWWWWWWW

WWWWWWWWWWWWWWWWWWWWWWWW
WWWW

I, PAULSON

OPPORTUNIST HEDGE FUND MANAGER

EXTRAORDINAIRE

In 2007, John Paulson made the mind-numbing sum of **$3.5 billion** at least in part by selling short on the collapsing United States home mortgage market. If this amount of money were averaged out over the entire year, it would mean that he made the following sums of money per time period:

$9,589,041 PER DAY

$67,123,287 PER WEEK

$287,671,230 PER MONTH

At **$9,589,041 PER DAY**, it is as if he won the lottery every single day for a year, or **365 lottery jackpots in a row**. Who needs Powerball when you can make more money by simply selling America short.

OPRAH WINFREY VS THE WORLD

It is difficult to believe that any single person could possess more wealth than an entire country produces in a year, but our bodacious band of billionaires has managed to pull it off.

Here are a few examples for your viewing pleasure. (Gross Domestic Product (GDP) is defined as the total output of goods and services produced by labor and property located within a country.)

Oprah Winfrey

Net Worth: **$2.7 BILLION**

Population: 1 person

Antigua and Barbuda

Population: 86,754

GDP: $1.5 BILLION

Cape Verde

Population: 508,659

GDP: $1.8 BILLION

Comoros

Population: 773,407

GDP: $765.8 MILLION

Djibouti

Population: 740,528

GDP: $2 BILLION

Dominica

Population: 78,813

GDP: $744.7 MILLION

The Gambia

Population: 1,824,158

GDP: $2.4 BILLION

Grenada

Population: 107,818

GDP: $1.1 BILLION

Guinea-Bissau

Population: 1,565,126

GDP: $1.7 BILLION

Kiribati

Population: 99,482

GDP: $602.2 MILLION

Liberia

Population: 3,685,076

GDP: $1.6 BILLION

Maldives

Population: 395,650

GDP: $1.7 BILLION

Marshall Islands

Population: 65,859

GDP: $133.5 MILLION

Micronesia

Population: 107,154

GDP: $238.1 MILLION

Monaco!!!

Population: 30,586

GDP: $976.3 MILLION

Nauru

Population: 9,267

GDP: $60 MILLION

Saint Kitts and Nevis

Population: 49,898

GDP: $725.8 MILLION

Saint Lucia

Population: 160,922

GDP: $1.7 BILLION

Saint Vincent and the Grenadines

Population: 104,217

GDP: $1.1 BILLION

Samoa

Population: 192,001

GDP: $1.04 BILLION

San Marino

Population: 31,477

GDP: $1.7 BILLION

Sao Tome and Principe

Population: 175,808

GDP: $295.1 MILLION

Seychelles

Population: 88,340

GDP: $1.8 BILLION

Solomon Islands

Population: 559,198

GDP: $1.5 BILLION

Tonga

Population: 122,580

GDP: $760.5 MILLION

Tuvalu

Population: 10,472

GDP: $14.9 MILLION

Vanuatu

Population: 221,552

GDP: $1.2 BILLION

<u>Zimbabwe</u>

Population: 11,651,858

GDP: <u>$98.1 MILLION</u>

<u>Palau</u>

Population: 20,879

GDP: <u>$164 MILLION</u>

As you can see, Oprah Winfrey, <u>ONE PERSON</u>, has a *greater net worth than* 28 INDIVIDUAL COUNTRIES' GDPs. Does this seem fair to you?

MICHAEL BLOOMBERG VS THE WORLD

Michael Bloomberg, the "King of New York", has such an unfathomable amount of money that he is worth more than the Gross Domestic Product of 67 individual

COUNTRIES. Here is a small sampling of the countries that he outdoes:

Michael Bloomberg

New Worth: **$19.5 BILLION**

Population: 1

The Bahamas

Population: 310,426

GDP: **$9.1 BILLION**

Haiti

Population: 9,648,924

GDP: **$12 BILLION**

Iceland

Population: 308,910

GDP: **$12.2 BILLION**

Liechtenstein

Population: 35,002

GDP: **$4.2 BILLION**

Mongolia

Population: 3,086,918

GDP: **$9.4 BILLION**

Nicaragua

Population: 5,995,928

GDP: **$16.5 BILLION**

Mega macro rich Bill Gates is so phenomenally loaded that he has more money than the Gross Domestic Product of

114 individual COUNTRIES. Here are a few examples:

Bill Gates

Net Worth: **$59 BILLION**

Population: 1

Bolivia

Population: 9,947,418

GDP: **$45.6 BILLION**

Estonia

Population: 1,291,170

GDP: $24 BILLION

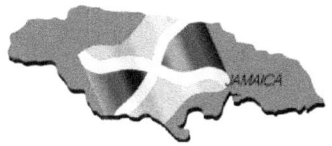

Jamaica

Population: 2,847,232

GDP: $23.8 BILLION

Lebanon

Population: 4,125,247

GDP: $54 BILLION

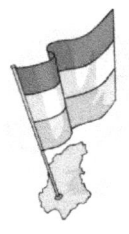

Luxembourg

Population: 497,538

GDP: $39.1 BILLION

Panama

Population: 3,410,676

GDP: $40.8 BILLION

Believe it or not, the combined net worth of the Forbes 400 Gang is greater than the Gross Domestic Product of a whopping 183 individual COUNTRIES. Here are just a few examples for your viewing pleasure: (Please bear in mind that there are only *195* nations *in the entire world.)*

The Forbes 400 Gang

Net Worth: $1.5 *TRILLION*

Population: 400

Argentina

Population: 41,343,201

GDP: $548.8 BILLION

($951 BILLION _LESS_ than

the Forbes 400 Gang)

<u>Australia</u>

Population: 21,515,754

GDP: <u>$851.1 BILLION</u>

($648 BILLION _LESS_ than

the Forbes 400 Gang)

<u>Austria</u>

Population: 8,214,160

GDP: <u>$321.8 BILLION</u>

($1.17 **TRILLION** _LESS_ than

the Forbes 400 Gang)

<u>Belgium</u>

Population: 10,423,493

GDP: <u>$383.4 BILLION</u>

($1.11 **TRILLION** LESS

than the Forbes 400 Gang)

<u>Colombia</u>

Population: 44,205,293

GDP: <u>$401.5 BILLION</u>

($1.1 **TRILLION** *LESS* than

the Forbes 400 Gang)

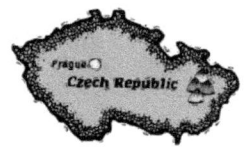

Czech Republic

Population: 10,201,707

GDP: $254.1 BILLION

($1.24 **TRILLION** LESS than

the Forbes 400 Gang)

Egypt

Population: 80,471,869

GDP: $469.8 BILLION

($1.03 **TRILLION** *LESS* than

the Forbes 400 Gang)

Greece

Population: 10,749,943

GDP: $333.4 BILLION

($1.16 **TRILLION** LESS than

the Forbes 400 Gang)

Ireland

Population: 4,622,917

GDP: $172.5 BILLION

($1.32 **TRILLION** *LESS* than

the Forbes 400 Gang)

Israel

Population: 7,353,985

GDP: $205.8 BILLION

($1.29 **TRILLION** LESS than

the Forbes 400 Gang)

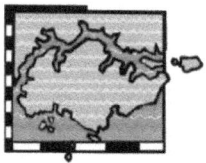

Singapore

Population: 4,701,069

GDP: $243.2 BILLION

($1.25 **TRILLION** *LESS* than

the Forbes 400 Gang)

<u>Switzerland</u>

Population: 7,623,438

GDP: <u>$314.7 BILLION</u>

($1.18 TRILLION LESS than

the Forbes 400 Gang)

If we compare the fortune of Michael Bloomberg, the King of New York City, to the Gross Domestic Products of the poorest countries on earth, we find that at $19.5 BILLION, Bloomberg's net worth surpasses the *CUMULATIVE* GDPs of the following countries:

<u>COUNTRY / GDP / POPULATION</u>

Antigua and Barbuda / <u>$1.5 Billion</u> / 86,754

Comoros / <u>$.77 Billion</u> / 773,407

Dominica / <u>$.74 Billion</u> / 72,813

Grenada / <u>$1.1   Billion</u> / 107,818

Kiribati / <u>$.60 Billion</u> / 99,482

Liberia / <u>$1.6   Billion</u> / 3,685,076

Maldives / <u>$1.7 Billion</u> / 395,650

Micronesia / <u>$.24 Billion</u> / 107,154

Monaco / <u>$.98 Billion</u> / 30,586

Nauru / <u>$.06 Billion</u> / 9,267

Palau / <u>$.16 Billion</u> / 20,879

Saint Kitts and Nevis / <u>$.73 Billion</u> / 49,898

Saint Lucia / $1.7 Billion / 160,922

Saint Vincent and the Grenadines / $1.1 Billion / 104,217

Samoa / $1.04 Billion / 192,001

San Marino / $1.7 Billion / 31,477

Sao Tome and Principe / $.30 Billion / 175,808

Solomon Islands / $1.5 Billion / 559,198

Tonga / $.76 Billion / 122,580

Tuvalu / $.01 Billion / 10,472

Vanuatu / $1.2 Billion / 221,552

Number of Countries: 21

Total Cumulative GDP: $19.49 Billion

Total Population: 7,017,011

Michael Bloomberg

Net Worth: $19.5 Billion

Population: 1 person

Oh, and by the way, the "poorest" member of the
Forbes Legalized Criminal
Organization (FLCO), a Mr. Dan Snyder
($1.05 Billion), is still worth more than the
GDPs of

13 Individual Countries

If Oprah Winfrey were compelled to spend her entire fortune of $2.7 billion in one year, she would have to spend the following amount of money each and every day to accomplish this herculean task:

$7,397,260

This means that by the end of the first week, she would have to spend:

$51,780,821

And by the end of the first month, she would have to spend:

$225,000,000

Wow, this is exhausting. Isn't it so much easier to simply be poor?

BILLIONAIRES HAVE THE

STRANGEST PROBLEMS

What is a multi-billionaire to do when he attempts to add up his 11-digit fortune, but his calculator only has a 10-digit display?

If the numbers don't fit,

your fortune's not legit.

Would somebody please make a calculator that will be of use to a multi-billionaire!

If your net worth is comprised of more digits than will fit on your calculator, you may be a greedy capitalist pig.

It has been estimated that Michael Bloomberg spent $100 million of his own money during his reelection campaign for mayor of New York City. This means that with his net worth of $19.5 billion, he could buy the following number of mayoral elections:

195 BOUGHT ELECTIONS

This means that if Michael Bloomberg happens to discover, or more likely buy, the fountain of youth, he could remain in office as the mayor of New York City for the next

780 YEARS

Or until the year

2791

The number of Americans living below the poverty line in 2008:

39.8 MILLION

The percentage of Americans living below the poverty line in 2008:

13.2%

The poverty-level cutoff for a family of four in 2008:

$22,025

The amount of money Oprah averaged every single hour of every single day from June 2007 to June 2008:

$31,392

The percentage of American children living below the poverty line in 2008:

18.5% or ALMOST ONE IN FIVE

The amount of time it took Oprah in June 2007 to June 2008 to make $22,025, the poverty-line income threshold for a family of four:

42 MINUTES

SPREADING THE WEALTH

If the total wealth of the Forbes 400 Gang were evenly distributed amongst the *poorest one million people* in the United States, each desperate poor person would receive a check for:

$1,500,000

This may very well be true, but it is obviously much more ethical and humane to have $1.5 TRILLION concentrated in only 400 sets of hands than in one million.

THE FORBES 400 MILITARY SUPERPOWER

If the Forbes 400 Gang decided to use their astronomical wealth to purchase weapons of mass destruction, they would possess one of the largest military forces on the face of the earth. Here is an example of what they could buy:

20 "Walton" Stealth Bombers @ $1 Billion each:

$20,000,000,000

100 "Bloomberg" F15k Fighter Bombers @ $100 million each:

$10,000,000,000

10 USS "Gates" Aircraft Carriers @$6.2 billion each:

$62,000,000,000

20 USS "Oprah Winfrey" Nuclear Submarines @ $1.8 billion each:

$36,000,000,000

100,000 Mercenary Soldiers @ $100,000 per year, per soldier:

$10,000,000,000

Total Cost: **$138 BILLION**

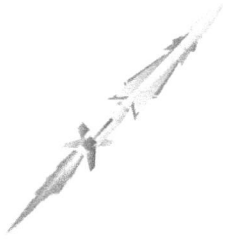

Hey, I was just thinking that with a military force of this size, they could proceed to take over the world if they so desired. Hold on. They already have taken over the world, haven't they?

Oh, and by the way, even after spending a mind-numbing **$138 Billion,** our beloved Forbes Gang would still be left with the tidy sum of $1.36 TRILLION.

TWO BILLION DOLLARS IS A

TERRIBLE THING TO WASTE

With tens of millions of Americans living in poverty, there are doubtlessly countless hungry and malnourished men, women, and children in the "Land of Plenty". With Donald Trump's massive storehouse of wealth, he could do a great deal to alleviate some of the hunger and suffering. If, for example, he would use just $2 billion of his $2.9 billion fortune to pay for meals and kept the remaining $900 million to scrape by on, he could feed the following number of desperate people, assuming that each meal costs $5:

EACH M̲ = 1 MILLION MEALS

MMMMMMMMMMMMMMMMMM
MMMMMMMMMMMMMMMMMM
MMMMMMMMMMMMMMMMMM
MMMMMMMMMMMMMMMMMM
MMMMMMMMMMMMMMMMMM
MMMMMMMMMMMMMMMMMM
MMMMMMMMMMMMMMMMMM
MMMMMMMMMMMMMMMMMM

MMMMMMMMMMMMMMMMMM
MMMMMMMMMMMMMMMMMM
MMMMMMMMMMMMMMMMMM
MMMMMMMMMMMMMMMMMM
MMMMMMMMMMMMMMMMMM
MMMMMMMMMMMMMMMMMM
MMMMMMMMMMMMMMMMMM
MMMMMMMMMMMMMMMMMM
MMMMMMMMMMMMMMMMMM
MMMMMMMMMMMMMMMMMM
MMMMMMMMMMMMMMMMMM
MMMMMMMMMMMMMMMMMM
MMMMMMMMMMMMMMMMMM
MMMMMMMMMMMMMMMMMM
MMMMMMMMMMMMMMMMMM
MMMMMMMM

For a total of *400 MILLION* Meals

BLOWN AWAY BY THOSE BILLIONAIRES

The estimated cost of the damages sustained by the ravages of Hurricane Katrina is somewhere in the vicinity of $108 billion. Admittedly, this is a staggering sum of money, but if every member of the Forbes 400 Legalized Criminal Organization would simply donate 10% of their net worth, it would more than cover this amount of money. In fact, 10% of the net worth of the Forbes 400 Gang comes out to $150 billion. This means that there would be $42 billion to spare, and our incredibly greedy billionaires would still be unimaginably wealthy.

Buck up you evil-minded bilkers. A stint in the Big House for financial fraud on a massive scale is no impediment to your dreams of one day possessing a towering mountain of filthy lucre. Look, this guy did it, and so can you!

Criminal's Name: Michael "Junk Bond" Milken

Crime: Multiple felony charges for violating

securities laws

Prison Sentence: 10 years

Time Served: *Less than 2 years*

Present Net Worth: **$2.1 BILLION**

Considering the magnitue of his crime, he acutally served very little jail time. Let us compare the punishment meeted out on Mr. Milken to that of your average unarmed bank robber:

Criminal's Name: Johnny Desperate

Crime: Unarmed bank robbery

Prison Sentence: 10 years

Time served: 6 years

Present Net Worth: Somewhere below $0

Given that the average amount of money stolen in a bank robbery is only $4,400, serving 6 years of a ten year sentence would equal one year served for every $734 stolen. If we assume that Mr. Milken made a mere $1 million through his illegal activities (it is, of course, more than likely that he made much, much more than this amount), this would mean that he served one year in prison for every illegally acquired $500,000.

Had Mr. Milken been required to serve the same amount of time per dollar stolen as our unarmed bank robber, he would have needed to remain in jail for 1,362 years.

The obvious moral of the story is that if you are hellbent on leading a life of crime, it is much safer and profitable to swindle a million dollars than a thousand. In other words, don't rob banks; become a Wall Street traitor instead.

THE KINDERGARTEN BILLIONAIRE CLUB

Hey gang, forget about having to work a lifetime to achieve unfathomable wealth because these guys prove that you can become a billionaire in practically no time at all.

Kindergarten Billionaire / Age / Undeserved Net Worth

Jerry Yang / 42 / $1.1 BILLION

Daniel Ziff / 39 / $4.2 BILLION

Larry Page / 38 / $16.7 BILLION

Sergey Brin / 38 / $16.7 BILLION

John Arnold / 37 / $3.5 BILLION

Dustin Moskovitz / 27 / $3.5 BILLION

But the undisputed, barely-legal kindergarten billionaire champion is:

Mark Zuckerberg / 27 / $17.5 BILLION

(He's slightly younger than his cohort, Mr. Moskovitz.)

This poor guy must have struggled his entire life, which amounts to only a few years, to achieve his staggering wealth. I guess this proves that putting in long hours and working hard have absolutely nothing to do with becoming fabulously rich.

In order for Mr. Zuckerberg to have reached $17.5 billion by his 27th birthday, the almost adolescent Facebook founder would have needed to average a massive $1.94 Billion each and every year since the time he reached 18 years of age and probably still in high school – private, elitist high school, of course. This works out to more than

$5.3 Million PER DAY.

MY HOME IS MY CASTLE, LITERALLY

The total net worth of the Forbes 400 Gang is

$1,500,000,000,000

This amount of money in one dollar bills could fill an area of

60,099,165 Cubic Feet

This means that their net worth in one dollar bills could fill the following number of 3,000 square foot homes with 9-foot ceilings:

EACH H = 1 HOME

HHHHHHHHHHHHHHHHHHHHHHHHHHH
HHHHHHHHHHHHHHHHHHHHHHHHHHH
HHHHHHHHHHHHHHHHHHHHHHHHHHH
HHHHHHHHHHHHHHHHHHHHHHHHHHH
HHHHHHHHHHHHHHHHHHHHHHHHHHH
HHHHHHHHHHHHHHHHHHHHHHHHHHH
HHHHHHHHHHHHHHHHHHHHHHHHHHH

HHHHHHHHHHHHHHHHHHHHHHHHH
HHHHHHHHHHHHHHHHHHHHHHHHH
HHHHHHHHHHHHHHHHHHHHHHHHH
HHHHHHHHHHHHHHHHHHHHHHHHH
HHHHHHHHHHHHHHHHHHHHHHHHH
HHHHHHHHHHHHHHHHHHHHHHHHH
HHHHHHHHHHHHHHHHHHHHHHHHH
HHHHHHHHHHHHHHHHHHHHHHHHH
HHHHHHHHHHHHHHHHHHHHHHHHH
HHHHHHHHHHHHHHHHHHHHHHHHH
HHHHHHHHHHHHHHHHHHHHHHHHH
HHHHHHHHHHHHHHHHHHHHHHHHH
HHHHHHHHHHHHHHHHHHHHHHHHH
HHHHHHHHHHHHHHHHHHHHHHHHH
HHHHHHHHHHHHHHHHHHHHHHHHH
HHHHHHHHHHHHHHHHHHHHHHHHH
HHHHHHHHHHHHHHHHHHHHHHHHH
HHHHHHHHHHHHHHHHHHHHHHHHH
HHHHHHHHHHHHHHHHHHHHHHHHH
HHHHHHHHHHHHHHHHHHHHHHHHH
HHHHHHHHHHHHHHHHHHHHHHHHH
HHHHHHHHHHHHHHHHHHHHHHHHH
HHHHHHHHHHHHHHHHHHHHHHHHH

HHHHHHHHHHHHHHHHHHHHHHHH
HHHHHHHHHHHHHHHHHHHHHHHH
HHHHHHHHHHHHHHHHHHHHHHHH
HHHHHHHHHHHHHHHHHHHHHHHH
HHHHHHHHHHHHHHHHHHHHHHHH
HHHHHHHHHHHHHHHHHHHHHHHH
HHHHHHHHHHHHHHHHHHHHHHHH
HHHHHHHHHHHHHHHHHHHHHHHH
HHHHHHHHHHHHHHHHHHHHHHHH
HHHHHHHHHHHHHHHHHHHHHHHH
HHHHHHHHHHHHHHHHHHHHHHHH
HHHHHHHHHHHHHHHHHHHHHHHH
HHHHHHHHHHHHHHHHHHHHHHHH
HHHHHHHHHHHHHHHHHHHHHHHH
HHHHHHHHHHHHHHHHHHHHHHHH
HHHHHHHHHHHHHHHHHHHHHHHH
HHHHHHHHHHHHHHHHHHHHHHHH
HHHHHHHHHHHHHHHHHHHHHHHH
HHHHHHHHHHHHHHHHHHHHHHHH
HHHHHHHHHHHHHHHHHHHHHHHH
HHHHHHHHHHHHHHHHHHHHHHHH
HHHHHHHHHHHHHHHHHHHHHHHH

HHHHHHHHHHHHHHHHHHHHHHHHH
HHHHHHHHHHHHHHHHHHHHHHHHH
HHHHHHHHHHHHHHHHHHHHHHHHH
HHHHHHHHHHHHHHHHHHHHHHHHH
HHHHHHHHHHHHHHHHHHHHHHHHH
HHHHHHHHHHHHHHHHHHHHHHHHH
HHHHHHHHHHHHHHHHHHHHHHHHH
HHHHHHHHHHHHHHHHHHHHHHHHH
HHHHHHHHHHHHHHHHHHHHHHHHH
HHHHHHHHHHHHHHHHHHHHHHHHH
HHHHHHHHHHHHHHHHHHHHHHHHH
HHHHHHHHHHHHHHHHHHHHHHHHH
HHHHHHHHHHHHHHHHHHHHHHHHH
HHHHHHHHHHHHHHHHHHHHHHHHH
HHHHHHHHHHHHHHHHHHHHHHHHH
HHHHHHHHHHHHHHHHHHHHHHHHH
HHHHHHHHHHHHHHHHHHHHHHHHH
HHHHHHHHHHHHHHHHHHHHHHHHH
HHHHHHHHHHHHHHHHHHHHHHHHH
HHHHHHHHHHHHHHHHHHHHHHHHH
HHHHHHHHHHHHHHHHHHHHHHHHH
HHHHHHHHHHHHHHHHHHHHHHHHH

HHHHHHHHHHHHHHHHHHHHHHHHHHHHHHH
HHHHHHHHHHHHHHHHHHHHHHHHHHHHHHH
HHHHHHHHHHHHHHHHHHHHHHHHHHHHHHH
HHHHHHHHHHHHHHHHHHHHHHHHHHHHHHH
HHHHHHHHHHHHHHHHHHHHHHHHHHHHHHH
HHHHHHHHHHHHHHHHHHHHHHHHHHHHHHH
HHHHHHHHHHHHHHHHHHHHHHHHHHHHHHH
HHHHHHHHHHHHHHHHHHHHHHHHHHHHHHH
HHHHHHHHHHHHHHHHHHHHHHHHHHHHHHH
HHHHHHHHHHHHHHHHHHHHHHHHHHHHHHH
HHHHHHHHHHHHHHHHHHHHHHHHHHHHHHH
HHHHHHHHHHHHHHHHHHHHHHHHHHHHHHH
HHHHHHHHHHHHHHHHHHHHHHHHHHHHHHH
HHHHHHHHHHHHHHHHHHHHHHHHHHHHHHH
HHHHHHHHHHHHHHHHHHHHHHHHHHHHHHH
HHHHHHHHHHHHHHHHHHHHHHHHHHHHHHH
HHHHHHHHHHHHHHHHHHHHHHHHH

Or

2,226 homes

Donald Trump, that loveable curmudgeon with the stylish coif, has a net worth of a cool $2.9 BILLION. If "Mr. Trump" decided that he would spend $72,000 per day on hair care products, it would take him

40,277 DAYS

or More Than

110 YEARS

before he would exhaust his $2.9 BILLION fortune.

This means that if he had begun to spend $72,000 EACH AND EVERY DAY starting in the year 1900, he would not have finished spending his last dollar until just prior to the year 2010. Presented below is the intrepid Trump's arduous attempt to empty his bank account:

YEAR

1900

AMOUNT SPENT

$0

YEAR

1902

THIS YEAR IN HISTORY

Teddy Roosevelt decides not to shoot a baby bear; he regrets the decision almost immediately.

YEAR

1923

THIS YEAR IN HISTORY

Flapper girls create disturbingly spastic dance routine.

YEAR

1931

THIS YEAR IN HISTORY

Hitler loses his mind.

YEAR

1940

AMOUNT SPENT

$1.05 BILLION

YEAR

1963

THIS YEAR IN HISTORY

The military industrial complex donates a brand new convertible to President Kennedy for his upcoming trip to Dallas.

YEAR

1978

THIS YEAR IN HISTORY

Al Gore invents the Internet.

YEAR

1980

AMOUNT SPENT

$2.1 BILLION

YEAR

1988

THIS YEAR IN HISTORY

George Bush enrolls in a "Hooked on Phonics" course. He drops out when the going gets "ruf".

YEAR

1992

THIS YEAR IN HISTORY

Bill Clinton becomes President in order to meet young girls.

YEAR

2002

THIS YEAR IN HISTORY

W.M.D. search commences in Iraq. One firecracker and a suspicious 12-gauge shotgun are discovered in Tikrit, thereby justifying invasion.

YEAR

2005

THIS YEAR IN HISTORY

Exxon becomes the largest company in the world; seizing Iraqi oil has nothing to do with its dramatic rise in profits.

YEAR

2008

THIS YEAR IN HISTORY

Donald Trump attempts to copyright the phrases "You're fired!", "Hello", and "Good Morning".

YEAR

2009

THIS YEAR IN HISTORY

Al Gore creates Facebook.

YEAR

2010

TOTAL AMOUNT SPENT

$2.9 BILLION

HIGH NOON

Michael Bloomberg, mayor of the mighty metropolis of New York City, has managed to rake in the unimaginably large sum of $19.5 BILLION in only 69 short years. If his net worth were averaged out evenly over his lifetime, he would have accumulated the following sums of money the *FIRST 12 HOURS OF HIS LIFE*:

MIDNIGHT: Baby Bloomberg is born

3 A.M.: $96,783 (Accumulated Wealth)

6 A.M.: $193,567 (Accumulated Wealth)

9 A.M.: $290,349 (Accumulated Wealth)

Noon: $387,135 (Accumulated Wealth)

This means that he would have needed to earn

$32,261 his FIRST HOUR of life

and

$774,270 by the end of the FIRST DAY

in order to reach $19.5 BILLION by his 69th birthday.

$19.5 billion dollars divided evenly over sixty-nine years comes out to over

$537 PER MINUTE

Here are the amounts of money the mighty Bloomberg needed to earn the *first 60 seconds* of his life in order to reach $19.5 BILLION by the age of 69:

5 Seconds Old : $44.75 (Accumulated Wealth)

10 Seconds Old : $89.50 (Accumulated Wealth)

15 Seconds Old : $134.25 (Accumulated Wealth)

20 Seconds Old : $179.00 (Accumulated Wealth)

25 Seconds Old : $223.75 (Accumulated Wealth)

30 Seconds Old : $268.50 (Accumulated Wealth)

35 Seconds Old : $313.25 (Accumulated Wealth)

40 Seconds Old : $358.00 (Accumulated Wealth)

45 Seconds Old : $\underline{\$402.75}$ (Accumulated Wealth)

50 Seconds Old : $\underline{\$447.50}$ (Accumulated Wealth)

55 Seconds Old : $\underline{\$492.25}$ (Accumulated Wealth)

60 Seconds Old : $\underline{\$537.00}$ (Accumulated Wealth)

BACK TO YOUR POST, SLAVE!

Since 1970 there has been a precipitous decline in work stoppages. As we all know, work stoppages or strikes are begun by workers in order to demand better pay, benefits and working conditions. This method of trying to obtain a living wage by the masses has been all but eradicated by the rich who own the companies. This, of course, is due to the ever-increasing power of the corporations and the ever-decreasing power of the workers and unions. Presented below are the disturbing statistics.

YEAR / WORK STOPPAGES

1970 / 381

1975 / 235

1980 / 187

1985 / 54

1990 / 44

1995 / 31

2000 / 39

2005 / 22

2006 / 20

2007 / 21

2008 / 15

2009 / 5

A giant sequoia in the Redwood National Park in California can reach a height of 311 feet. If **one billion dollars** in one dollar bills were stacked next to each giant sequoia with a height of 311 feet, there would stacks of money reaching the tops of

1,152 Trees

And the total height of the 1,152 stacks of one dollar bills would be

358,300 Feet

Meanwhile, Warren Buffett's net worth of $39 BILLION would be stacked next to

44,928 311-Foot Sequoia Trees

and would reach a total height of

13,973,700 Feet

"Preferring to store her money in the stomachs of the needy rather than hide it in a purse."

-Saint Jerome

A loathsome, liberal do-gooder

"Ketchup is a vegetable."

-President Ronald Reagan

If a billionaire were told that he only had one year to live and he decided to really live it up by spending $100,000 per day over the next 365-day period, by the end of the year, he would still be left with

$963 MILLION

of his billion-dollar fortune.

This means that even after blowing $100,000 *every single day of the year*, he will have spent only

$36.5 Million

or only

3.65%.

of his billion dollar fortune.

On the following pages, we shall see how our courageous and intrepid billionaire might decide to spend

$100,000 *per day* in a valiant but hopelessly vain attempt to empty his bank account in only one year.

A REALLY, REALLY, REALLY BIG BUCKET LIST

DAY ONE

OFF TO MERRY OLD ENGLAND

First-class flight for 2 from N.Y.C. to London: $11,517

One night in the Royal Suite, Intercontinental Park Lane hotel: $17,500

Donation to the "Billionaire Relief Fund*": $70,983

Total: $100,000

AMOUNT OF $1 BILLION REMAINING:

$999,900,000

AMOUNT SPENT

$100,000

PERCENT OF $1 BILLION SPENT:

.01% (one one-hundredth of one percent)

PERCENT OF $1 BILLION REMAINING:

99.99%

*The Billionaire Relief Fund is a for-profit organization created by our hypothetical billionaire to ensure that retired billionaires are always provided with life's bare necessities, such as discounts on Lamborghinis, complementary meals at the White House, and guaranteed membership at the yearly *"Let's Worship Father Satan Festival"* in Bohemian Meadows, California.

A REALLY, REALLY, REALLY BIG BUCKET LIST

DAY FOUR

GET YOUR MOTOR RUNNIN'

Cadillac CTS-V: $60,700

Harley Davidson Sportster 883 Low: 3 @ $7,500: $22,500

Donation to the Billionaire Relief Fund: $16,800

Day Three Total: $100,000

AMOUNT OF $1 BILLION REMAINING

$999,600,000

CUMULATIVE AMOUNT SPENT

(Days 1 through 4)

$400,000

PERCENT OF $1 BILLION SPENT

.04% (one four-hundredths of one percent)

PERCENT OF $1 BILLION REMAINING

99.96%

A REALLY, REALLY, REALLY BIG BUCKET LIST

DAY 10

JEEVES, I BELIEVE WE'RE OUT OF AMANTILLADO!

Le Macchiole 2005 Messorio: 10 @ $320: **$3,200**

Mas de Boislouzon 2006 Chateauneuf-

Du-Pape "Quet": 10 @ $60: **$600**

Vina Cobas 2005 uNico Mendoza: 10 @ $200: $2,000

Pierre Morey 2006 Meursault Perrieres

Premier Cru: 10 @ $170: $1,700

Highland Park 40-Year-Old Single

Malt Whisky: 10 @ $2,000: $20,000

Pierre Ferrand Single Vintage Cognac: 10 @ $1,500: $15,000

AsomBroso Vintage Extra Anejo Tequila: 10 @ $1,100: $11,000

Moet & Chandon Champagne Cuvve

Dom Perignon Rose 1995: 10 @ $1,200: $12,000

Donation to Billionaire Relief Fund: $34,500

Day Ten Total: $100,000

AMOUNT OF $1 BILLION REMAINING:

$999,000,000

CUMULATIVE AMOUNT SPENT

(Days 1 through 10)

$1,000,000

PERCENT OF $1 BILLION SPENT:

.1% (one tenth of one percent)

PERCENT OF $1 BILLION REMAINING:

99.9%

A REALLY, REALLY, REALLY BIG BUCKET LIST

DAY 53

EVERY WOMAN'S CRAZY ABOUT A SHARP DRESSED BILLIONAIRE

Cesare Attolini Charcoal Suit: $5,100

Cesare Attolini Brown & Ivory Cream Suit: $5,100

Borrelli Gray Suit: $4,200

Borrelli Khaki Suit: $4,200

Kiton Navy Blue Suit: $6,300

Kiton Brown Suit: $5,700

Kiton Cotton Shirts, various colors: 10 @ $1,100: $11,000

Kiton Silk Ties: 10 @ $250: $2,500

Rolex Yacht-Master Men's Watch: $37,150

Donation to the Billionaire Relief Fund: $18,750

Day 53 Total: $100,000

AMOUNT OF $1 BILLION REMAINING:

$994,700,000

CUMULATIVE AMOUNT SPENT

(Days 1 through 53)

$5,300,000

PERCENT OF $1 BILLION SPENT:

.53% (fifty-three hundredths of

one percent)

PERCENT OF $1 BILLION REMAINING:

99.47%

A REALLY, REALLY, REALLY BIG BUCKET LIST

DAY 68

BABY NEEDS A NEW PAIR OF DIAMOND EARRINGS

Harry Winston Short Drop Diamond Earrings: $25,000

Harry Winston Diamond Tennis Bracelet: $21,000

Harry Winston Four Row Diamond Ring: $12,800

Harry Winston Diamond Cluster Pendant: $19,000

Harry Winston Diamond and Mother of Pearl Cufflinks: $21,000

Donation to the Billionaire Relief Fund: $1,200

Day 68 Total: $100,000

AMOUNT OF $1 BILLION REMAINING

$993,200,000

CUMULATIVE AMOUNT SPENT

(Days 1 through 68)

$6,800,000

.68% (sixty-eight hundredths of one percent)

PERCENT OF $1 BILLION REMAINING

99.32%

A REALLY, REALLY, REALLY BIG BUCKET LIST

DAY 144

A VIPER FOR A SNAKE

Dodge Viper Convertible: $90,000

Donation to the Billionaire Relief Fund: $10,000

Day 144 Total: $100,000

AMOUNT OF $1 BILLION REMAINING:

$985,600,000

(Days 1 through 144)

$14,400,000

PERCENT OF $1 BILLION SPENT:

1.44%

PERCENT OF $1 BILLION REMAINING:

98.56%

A REALLY, REALLY, REALLY BIG BUCKET LIST

DAY 199

EINE KLEINE NACHTMUSIK

New Steinway Grand Piano: $76,000

Donation to the Billionaire Relief Fund: $24,000

Day 199 Total: $100,000

AMOUNT OF $1 BILLION REMAINING:

$980,100,000

CUMULATIVE AMOUNT SPENT

(Days 1 through 199)

$19,900,000

PERCENT OF $1 BILLION SPENT:

1.99%

PERCENT OF $1 BILLION REMAINING:

98.01%

A REALLY, REALLY, REALLY BIG BUCKET LIST

DAY 365

THE DAY OF RECKONING

The day that our spendthrift billionaire has dreaded over the past year has finally arrived, but to his complete and utter astonishment his battalion of the best doctors money can buy has just informed him that there has been a miraculous turnaround in his medical condition. As a matter of fact, they believe that he could live another fifty years or so in perfect health. After his initial elation, his thoughts immediately return to the amount of money he has blown over the past year. He has his accountants perform the calculations. Here are the results:

TOTAL AMOUNT SPENT

(Days 1 through 365))

$36,500,000

AMOUNT OF $1 BILLION REMAINING:

$963,500,000

PERCENT OF $1 BILLION SPENT:

3.65%

PERCENT OF $1 BILLION REMAINING:

96.35%

Even after an *entire year* of spending
$100,000 *each and every day*, he
has barely even put a dent into his fortune.

His accountants inform him that his worries of blowing his fortune are unfounded because in order for him to spend his entire $1 billion fortune, he would have to spend

$100,000 *each and every day for the next* 27.4 YEARS.

So relieved and overjoyed is our healthy plutocrat that he decides to throw a lavish $7 million Arabia Nights themed party in Marrakesh, Morocco. In order to pay for this extravagance, he fires one-third of his multinational company's employees and eliminates healthcare coverage for the remaining rank and file workers. Life is good.

BILLIONAIRES JUST WANT TO HAVE FUN

NOT FEED THE STARVING MASSES

A bottle of Dom Perignon White Gold Jeroboam once sold for $40,000. (Probably to some billionaire who happened to be really thirsty but couldn't find a coke machine to satisfy his jaded thirst.)

The money spent on that *one bottle of champagne* could have instead been spent on the following number of loaves of bread for the starving children:

(Assuming $2 per loaf)

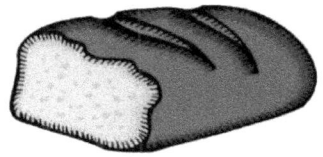

20,000 LOAVES OF BREAD

As we the masses ride the capitalist economic roller coaster down the hill towards financial hell, our intrepid billionaires have no fear. In fact, they have never had it so good. Of the 400 richest Americans, *only 39* saw their fortunes decrease from 2009 to 2010. In fact, most of the richest people in America saw their fortunes *SOAR* between 2009 and 2010. All of this during a global economic recession.

Presented below is an illustration of the precipitous increase in the number of parasitic, blood-sucking billionaires in the United States from 2009 to 2010:

NUMBER OF BILLIONAIRES IN THE U.S.

2009

359

2010

403

INCREASE

12.3%

TOTAL NET WORTH

$1.349 TRILLION

During the same time period, the number of people *living in poverty* SKYROCKETED from over 43 MILLION people to over 46 MILLION people, a 6% increase in just one year.

This is what is known as "The Rich Get Richer While the Poor Get Poorer" or more specifically what is known as the "Parasite Effect" in microeconomic theory. It is also known as the "Masses Doing Most of the Work and the Elite Obtaining Most of the Profits".

ONE BILLION AND COUNTING,

AND COUNTING...

If you happened to be a miserly old billionaire who was obsessed with counting your endless stacks of paper money, it would take the following length of time to count $1 BILLION in one dollar bills if you counted one dollar *per second*:

31.7 YEARS

This means that if you had started to count your money on June 1, 1978, you would not have reached $1 billion until January 1, 2010. This would have taken you through the following Presidential administrations:

Half of the JIMMY CARTER ADMINISTRATION

(*and counting*)

The RONALD REAGAN ADMINISTRATION

(*and counting*)

The GEORGE H.W. BUSH ADMINISTRATION

(*and counting*)

The BILL CLINTON ADMINISTRATION

(and counting)

The GEORGE W. BUSH ADMINISTRATION

(and counting)

And into

The BARAK OBAMA ADMINISTRATION

As a comparison, if you happen to earn $50,000 per year, it would take you the following length of time to count this amount of money in one dollar bills if you counted one dollar per second:

13.9 HOURS

This means that if you started to count your money at midnight, you would reach $50,000 by 1:54 P.M. of the

SAME DAY

Hey, this still leaves you enough time to catch some programs on the OWN Network. Lucky you.

THE *RACE* TO $19.5 BILLION

THE COMPETITORS:

CHIP THE PAINTER ($50,000 per year)

Time needed to earn $19.5 BILLION

390,000 YEARS

VS.

MICHAEL BLOOMBERG

Time needed to earn $19.5 BILLION

Less than 69 YEARS

Presented below is a timeline of their respective journeys to $19.5 BILLION.

CHIP THE PAINTER = C

EACH C = 1,000 YEARS OF WORK

MICHAEL BLOOMBERG = B

EACH B = 69 YEARS OF "WORK"

DON'T BLINK. THIS COULD BE CLOSE

GO!

387,990 B.C. to 327,990 B.C.

cccccccccccccccccccccccccccccccccccccccccccccccccccccccccccccc

Accumulated Wealth: Chip: $3 Billion

Chip has worked 60,000 years to reach the $3 billion mark.

Bloomberg has not yet begun to earn his billions.

327,990 B.C. to 267,990 B.C.

cccccccccccccccccccccccccccccccccccccccccccccccccccccccccccccc

Accumulated Wealth: Chip: $6 Billion

Chip has now been working 120,000 years to reach the

$6 billion mark.

Bloomberg has not yet begun to earn his many billions.

267,990 B.C. to 207,990 B.C.

cccccccccccccccccccccccccccccccccccccccccccccccccccccccccccccc

(Remember, each "c" represents 1000 years of work for Chip.)

Accumulated Wealth: Chip: $9 Billion

Chip has put in 180,000 years of back-breaking labor to earn $9 Billion.

Bloomberg has not yet begun to earn his $19.5 Billion fortune.

207,990 B.C. to 147,990 B.C.

cccccccccccccccccccccccccccccccccccccccccccccccccccccccccccc

Accumulated Wealth: Chip: $12 Billion

Believe it or not, Chip has had to work 240,000 years to earn $12 Billion.

Bloomberg has not yet begun to earn his massive fortune.

147,990 B.C. to 87,990 B.C.

cccccccccccccccccccccccccccccccccccccccccccccccccccccccccccc

Accumulated Wealth: Chip: $15 Billion

Chip has now ceaselessly slaved away for 300,000 years in order to reach $15 Billion.

Bloomberg has not yet begun to earn his billions.

<u>87,990 B.C. to 27,990 B.C.</u>

cccccccccccccccccccccccccccccccccccccccccccccccccccccccccccc

Accumulated Wealth: Chip: $18 Billion

Poor Chip is on the precipice of death after

360,000 years of labor.

Bloomberg has not yet begun to earn his astronomical fortune.

<u>27,990 B.C. to 2010 A.D.</u>

cccccccccccccccccccccccccccccc

B

Bloomberg's "B" represents less than 69 years of "work" to reach $19.5 Billion. Each "c" represents 1000 years of work for Chip.

Accumulated Wealth:

Chip: $19.5 Billion

Bloomberg: $19.5 Billion

Bloomberg didn't need to start to make his $19.5 BILLION FORTUNE until the year <u>1942</u>, 389,931 YEARS <u>after</u> poor old Chip began.

(It should be mentioned that, in John Henry-like fashion, exhausted Chip passed out head first into a five-gallon bucket of high gloss enamel paint and drowned to death at the exact moment he reached $19.5 billion. This unfortunate turn of events occurred after 390,000 years of backbreaking work.)

"It is easier for a camel to pass through the eye of a needle than for a rich man to enter the gates of heaven."

-Matthew 19:24

The Holy Bible

"All we are saying is give greed a chance."

-Humble, heartfelt request of

the Forbes 400 Gang

LOOK MA,

I'VE GOT MORE MONEY THAN A BANK!

In the United States, there are 8,012 FDIC-insured financial institutions. These banks have total assets of $13,019,000,000,000. Of these 8,012 banks, 7,340 have assets of $1 billion or less. This means that with a net worth of $2.7 billion, Oprah is worth more than _at least_ 7,340 (or 92%) of the 8,012 FDIC-insured financial institutions in the U.S.

Of the 8,012 FDIC-insured commercial banks and savings institutions, 7,905 have assets of $10 billion or less. This means that with a net worth of $19.5 billion, Bloomberg is worth more than _at least_ 7,905 (98.6%) of the 8,012 FDIC-insured financial institutions in the United States.

<u>LOOK MA,</u>

<u>I'VE GOT MORE MONEY THAN A BANK!</u>

(PART II)

I know that it is inconceivable that anyone could actually possess more money than a bank, but our beloved billionaires have managed to pull off this incredible feat. Here are just a few examples:

IN THIS CORNER:

<u>WARREN BUFFETT</u>

NET ASSETS: $39 BILLION

HIS OPPONENT:

<u>FIRST NATIONAL OF NEBRASKA</u>

TOTAL ASSETS: $17 BILLION

AND THE WINNER IS:

<u>WARREN BUFFETT</u>

BY $22 BILLION

IN THIS CORNER:

OPRAH WINFREY

NET ASSETS: $2.7 BILLION

HER OPPONENT:

FIRST STATE BANK OF CHICAGO

TOTAL ASSETS: $219.2 MILLION

AND THE WINNER IS:

OPRAH WINFREY

BY $2.48 BILLION

THE FIRST NATIONAL BANK OF BLOOMBERG

With a net worth of $19.5 BILLION, Mayor Bloomberg could write a check of more than $2,323 to each and every of the 8,391,881 residents of the fair metropolis of New York City

I'm not a doctor, but I think he most probably would develop carpal tunnel syndrome after signing this many checks.

THE FORBES 400 GANG

VS.

THE LARGEST BANK IN THE UNITED STATES

THE FORBES 400 GANG'S TOTAL ASSETS

$1,500,000,000,000

That's One **TRILLION**!!!

Five hundred **BILLION**!!

VS

THE LARGEST BANK IN THE UNITED STATES:

BANK OF AMERICA

TOTAL DEPOSITS

$916 BILLION

AND THE UNDISPUTED WINNER IS:

THE FORBES 400 GANG

BY $584 BILLION

It wasn't even close, was it?

DEEP THOUGHTS

THOUGHT # 1

If Michael Bloomberg, the King of New York, won a lottery jackpot of $1 million, would it be worth his time to claim such a paltry sum? After all, $19.5 billion, his net worth, is *19,500 times greater* than one million dollars.

This is the relative equivalent of someone with a net worth of $200,000 winning a lottery jackpot of *$10.26*

THOUGHT #2

If King Bloomberg were strolling down a street in New York City and some spare change, let's say $100,000, fell out of his Armani Cashmere overcoat into a mud puddle, would he fish it out of the murky water?

After all, $100,000 to King Bloomberg is the relative equivalent of $1.03 to a person with a net worth of $200,000.

In both of the cases presented above, Bloomberg would enlist the services of some desperate rummy - paying him minimum wage of course - to secure his funds for him. Let it be understood that said desperate rummy would not be compensated for any soiled garments that might result from wallowing in a pool of muddy water.

WORKIN' IN A COAL MINE

The average weekly salary for a coal miner in 2009 was $1,249, which comes to $64,948 for a year's work. If a coal miner worked for 40 years at this rate of pay, he would earn $2,597,920 over his career.

The amount of time it took Oprah to make $2.6 million from June 2007 - June 2008:

3.5 DAYS

From June 2007 – June 2008, Oprah made $275 MILLION. As such, it took her only

2 HOURS

to make $64,948, the average yearly salary of a coal miner.

However, one must take into consideration that she did put in ten-hour days.

One billion dollars in one dollar bills could fill the following number of briefcases with dimension of 18" x 13" x 4"

73,717 BRIEFCASES

By comparison, someone with the substantial net worth of $500,000 could only fill 37 Briefcases

While Donald Trump's net worth of $2.9 Billion could fill

213,779 BRIEFCASES

BELIEVE IT OR NOT

The number of people below the poverty line has increased from 31.6 million in the year 2000 to 39.8 million in 2008, an increase of 8.2 million people, or 25.9% over an eight-year period.

Despite this precipitous rise in poverty, the number of billionaires over the same time period *increased* by *957%!*

These crooked capitalists can't lose. When the masses are up, they're up. When the masses are down, they're up.

Presented below is a table showing this unusual relationship between the super-rich and everyone else.

NUMBER OF PEOPLE

BELOW THE POVERTY LINE

2000: 31.6 MILLION

2008: 39.8 MILLION

INCREASE: 25.9%

NUMBER OF BILLIONAIRES

2000:

49

2008:

469

INCREASE: 957%

From June 2007 to June 2008, the unsinkable Oprah Winfrey made a whopping $275 million. This modest sum works out to

$753,424 PER DAY

or

$31,392 PER HOUR.

A dump truck driver who earns $35,000 per year would have to work

7,847 DAYS

Or

21.5 YEARS

to earn as much as the selfless Oprah earned in only *ONE DAY* in 2007-2008.

Moreover, in a one-week period in 2007-2008, Oprah made on average $5,273,968. In order for the

$35,000-per-year dump truck driver to earn this amount of money, our exhausted driver would have to work

55,005 DAYS

Or

150.7 YEARS

IMAGINE NO BILLIONAIRES

IT'S EASY IF YOU TRY

If everyone who made the Forbes 400 Legalized Criminal Organization, the FLCO, were reduced in wealth to a meager, subsistence level of $100 million each, they would lose $1,460,000,000,000 of their $1,500,000,000,000 fortune or 97% of their combined net worth.

The United States (the richest country in the history of "civilization"), has a population of 307 million people. If $1,460,000,000,000 were distributed evenly to *each and every citizen* of the U.S., *each person* would receive a check for $4,755.70

But let's be realistic for a moment. Although distributing the wealth amongst the hundreds of millions of people in our country may be a noble cause, we all know that our greedy billionaires are not about to relinquish their fortunes to the lowly masses. Beside, can a plutocrat actually survive on a mere $100 million these days? Our beloved billionaires certainly don't think so.

Oprah Winfrey's net worth of $2.7 billion in one dollar bills could fill

108,178 CUBIC FEET

This means that her massive wealth could completely fill a building from floor to ceiling that is

100 feet long

100 feet wide

and with a

10 foot 9 inch ceiling

SLUMDOG BILLIONAIRE

If Oprah went slumming and decided to buy some "low-income" houses at $100,000 a pop, she could purchase the following number of houses with her $2.7 billion fortune:

EACH H = 10 HOUSES

HHHHHHHHHHHHHHHHHHHHHHHHHHHHHHH
HHHHHHHHHHHHHHHHHHHHHHHHHHHHHHH
HHHHHHHHHHHHHHHHHHHHHHHHHHHHHHH
HHHHHHHHHHHHHHHHHHHHHHHHHHHHHHH
HHHHHHHHHHHHHHHHHHHHHHHHHHHHHHH
HHHHHHHHHHHHHHHHHHHHHHHHHHHHHHH
HHHHHHHHHHHHHHHHHHHHHHHHHHHHHHH
HHHHHHHHHHHHHHHHHHHHHHHHHHHHHHH
HHHHHHHHHHHHHHHHHHHHHHHHHHHHHHH
HHHHHHHHHHHHHHHHHHHHHHHHHHHHHHH
HHHHHHHHHHHHHHHHHHHHHHHHHHHHHHH
HHHHHHHHHHHHHHHHHHHHHHHHHHHHHHH
HHHHHHHHHHHHHHHHHHHHHHHHHHHHHHH
HHHHHHHHHHHHHHHHHHHHHHHHHHHHHHH
HHHHHHHHHHHHHHHHHHHHHHHHHHHHHHH
HHHHHHHHHHHHHHHHHHHHHHHHHHHHHHH
HHHHHHHHHHHHHHHHHHHHHHHHHHHHHHH
HHHHHHHHHHHHHHHHHHHHHHHHHHHHHHH

HHHHHHHHHHHHHHHHHHHHHHHHHHHHHHHH
HHHHHHHHHHHHHHHHHHHHHHHHHHHHHHHH
HHHHHHHHHHHHHHHHHHHHHHHHHHHHHHHH
HHHHHHHHHHHHHHHHHHHHHHHHHHHHHHHH
HHHHHHHHHHHHHHHHHHHHHHHHHHHHHHHH
HHHHHHHHHHHHHHHHHHHHHHHHHHHHHHHH
HHHHHHHHHHHHHHHHHHHHHHHHHHHHHHHH
HHHHHHHHHHHHHHHHHHHHHHHHHHHHHHHH
HHHHHHHHHHHHHHHHHHHHHHHHHHHHHHHH
HHHHHHHHHHHHHHHHHHHHHHHHHHHHHHHH
HHHHHHHHHHHHHHHHHHHHHHHHHHHHHHHH
HHHHHHHHHHHHHHHHHHHHHHHHHHHHHHHH
HHHHHHHHHHHHHHHHHHHHHHHHHHHHHHHH
HHHHHHHHHHHHHHHHHHHHHHHHHHHHHHHH
HHHHHHHHHHHHHHHHHHHHHHHHHHHHHHHH
HHHHHHHHHHHHHHHHHHHHHHHHHHHHHHHH
HHHHHHHHHHHHHHHHHHHHHHHHHHHHHHHH
HHHHHHHHHHHHHHHHHHHHHHHHHHHHHHHH
HHHHHHHHHHHHHHHHHHHHHHHHHHHHHHHH
HHHHHHHHHHHHHHHHHHHHHHHHHHHHHHHH
HHHHHHHHHHHHHHHHHHHHHHHHHHHHHHHH
HHHHHHHHHHHHHHHHHHHHHHHHHHHHHHHH
HHHHHHHHHHHHHHHHHHHHHHHHHHHHHHHH
HHHHHHHHHHHHHHHHHHHHHHHHHHHHHHHH
HHHHHHHHHHHHHHHHHHHHHHHHHHHHHHHH
HHHHHHHHHHHHHHHHHHHHHHHHHHHHHHHH
HHHHHHHHHHHHHHHHHHHHHHHHHHHHHHHH
HHHHHHHHHHHHHHHHHHHHHHHHHHHHHHHH
HHHHHHHHHHHHHHHHHHHHHHHHHHHHHHHH

HHHHHHHHHHHHHHHHHHHHHHHHHHHHHH
HHHHHHHHHHHHHHHHHHHHHHHHHHHHHH
HHHHHHHHHHHHHHHHHHHHHHHHHHHHHH
HHHHHHHHHHHHHHHHHHHHHHHHHHHHHH
HHHHHHHHHHHHHHHHHHHHHHHHHHHHHH
HHHHHHHHHHHHHHHHHHHHHHHHHHHHHH
HHHHHHHHHHHHHHHHHHHHHHHHHHHHHH
HHHHHHHHHHHHHHHHHHHHHHHHHHHHHH
HHHHHHHHHHHHHHHHHHHHHHHHHHHHHH
HHHHHHHHHHHHHHHHHHHHHHHHHHHHHH
HHHHHHHHHHHHHHHHHHHHHHHHHHHHHH
HHHHHHHHHHHHHHHHHHHHHHHHHHHHHH
HHHHHHHHHHHHHHHHHHHHHHHHHHHHHH
HHHHHHHHHHHHHHHHHHHHHHHHHHHHHH
HHHHHHHHHHHHHHHHHHHHHHHHHHHHHH
HHHHHHHHHHHHHHHHHHHHHHHHHHHHHH
HHHHHHHHHHHHHHHHHHHHHHHHHHHHHH
HHHHHHHHHHHHHHHHHHHHHHHHHHHHHH
HHHHHHHHHHHHHHHHHHHHHHHHHHHHHH
HHHHHHHHHHHHHHHHHHHHHHHHHHHHHH
HHHHHHHHHHHHHHHHHHHHHHHHHHHHHH
HHHHHHHHHHHHHHHHHHHHHHHHHHHHHH
HHHHHHHHHHHHHHHHHHHHHHHHHHHHHH
HHHHHHHHHHHHHHHHHHHHHHHHHHHHHH
HHHHHHHHHHHHHHHHHHHHHHHHHHHHHH
HHHHHHHHHHHHHHHHHHHHHHHHHHHHHH
HHHHHHHHHHHHHHHHHHHHHHHHHHHHHH

HHHHHHHHHHHHHHHHHHHHHHHHHHHHHHHHHHHHHH
HHHHHHHHHHHHHHHHHHHHHHHHHHHHHHHHHHHHHH
HHHHHHHHHHHHHHHHHHHHHHHHHHHHHHHHHHHHHH
HHHHHHHHHHHHHHHHHHHHHHHHHHHHHHHHHHHHHH
HHHHHHHHHHHHHHHHHHHHHHHHHHHHHHHHHHHHHH
HHHHHHHHHHHHHHHHHHHHHHHHHHHHHHHHHHHHHH
HHHHHHHHHHHHHHHHHHHHHHHHHHHHHHHHHHHHHH
HHHHHHHHHHHHHHHHHHHHHHHHHHHHHHHHHHHHHH
HHHHHHHHHHHHHHHHHHHHHHHHHHHHHHHHHHHHHH
HHHHHHHHHHHHHHHHHHHHHHHHHHHHHHHHHHHHHH
HHHHHHHHHHHHHHHHHHHHHHHHHHHHHHHHHHHHHH
HHHHHHHHHHHHHHHHHHHHHHHHHHHHHHHHHHHHHH
HHHHHHHHHHHHHHHHHHHHHHHHHHHHHHHHHHHHHH
HHHHHHHHHHHHHHHHHHHHHHHHHHHHHHHHHHHHHH
HHHHHHHHHHHHHHHHHHHHHHHHHHHHHHHHHHHHHH
HHHHHHHHHHHHHHHHHHHHHHHHHHHHHHHHHHHHHH
HHHHHHHHHHHHHHHHHHHHHHHHHHHHHHHHHHHHHH
HHHHHHHHHHHHHHHHHHHHHHHHHHHHHHHHHHHHHH
HHHHHHHHHHHHHHHHHHHHHHHHHHHHHHHHHHHHHH
HHHHHHHHHHHHHHHHHHHHHHHHHHHHHHHHHHHHHH
HHHHHHHHHHHHHHHHHHHHHHHHHHHHHHHHHHHHHH
HHHHHHHHHHHHHHHHHHHHHHHHHHHHHHHHHHHHHH
HHHHHHHHHHHHHHHHHHHHHHHHHHHHHHHHHHHHHH
HHHHHHHHHHHHH

Which comes to

<u>27,000</u> $100,000 homes.

If Warren Buffett decided that he needed a few safe houses in which to hold up in the event that the hypnotized masses ever awaken from their somnambulistic stupor and demand a more equitable distribution of the wealth, he could purchase the following number of $5 million Fifth Avenue and Park Avenue apartments with his modest $39 billion fortune:

EACH A = 10 apartments

AAAAAAAAAAAAAAAAAAAA
AAAAAAAAAAAAAAAAAAAA
AAAAAAAAAAAAAAAAAAAA
AAAAAAAAAAAAAAAAAAAA
AAAAAAAAAAAAAAAAAAAA
AAAAAAAAAAAAAAAAAAAA
AAAAAAAAAAAAAAAAAAAA
AAAAAAAAAAAAAAAAAAAA

AAAAAAAAAAAAAAAAAAAAA

AAAAAAAAAAAAAAAAAAAAA

AAAAAAAAAAAAAAAAAAAAA

AAAAAAAAAAAAAAAAAAAAA

AAAAAAAAAAAAAAAAAAAAA

AAAAAAAAAAAAAAAAAAAAA

AAAAAAAAAAAAAAAAAAAAA

AAAAAAAAAAAAAAAAAAAAA

AAAAAAAAAAAAAAAAAAAAA

AAAAAAAAAAAAAAAAAAAAA

AAAAAAAAAAAAAAAAAAAAA

AAAAAAAAAAAAAAAAAAAAA

AAAAAAAAAAAAAAAAAAAAA

AAAAAAAAAAAAAAAAAAAAA

AAAAAAAAAAAAAAAAAAAAA

AAAAAAAAAAAAAAAAAAAAA

AAAAAAAAAAAAAAAAAAAAA

AAAAAAAAAAAAAAAAAAAAA

AAAAAAAAAAAAAAAAAAAA
AAAAAAAAAPARTMEAAAAAAAA
AAAAAAAAAAAAAAAAAAAA
AAAAAAAAAAAAAAAAAAAA
AAAAAAAAAAAAAAAAAAAA
AAAAAAAAAAAAAAAAAAAA
AAAAAAAAAAAAAAAAAAAA
AAAAAAAAAAAAAAAAAAAA
AAAAAAAAAAAAAAAAAAAA
AAAAAAAAAAAAAAAAAAAA
AAAAAAAAAAAAAAAAAAAA
AAAAAAAAAAAAAAAAAAAA
AAAAAAAAAAAAAAAAAAAA
AAAAAAAAAAAAAAAAAAAA

Or

7,800 $5 MILLION
APARTMENTS

WELCOME TO BUFFETTOWN

You can check out any time you like,

but you can never leave.

A family with a net worth of $250,000 may think that they are doing well financially, but Warren Buffett, with a ridiculously gargantuan net worth of $39 billion, is worth

156,000 TIMES MORE

than the family worth $250,000

This means that if there were a city with a population close to 156,000 people – let's say Savannah, Georgia (population 136,286) – and each person in this city had a net worth of $250,000, Warren Buffett, ONE SOLITARY PERSON, would be worth MORE than all of the people in this city COMBINED.

Let us conclude our examination of the super-rich with the richest of the rich, Bill Gates. I am sure that the vast majority of the people in the United States would think that $1 million is a substantial amount of money. However, in relation to the wealth possessed by our beloved billionaire, Mr. Gates, this amounts to little more than petty cash. As an illustrative example, Bill Gates' net worth of $59 billion in relation to someone with a net worth of $1 million would be represented as presented below:

Each $ = $1 million

SOMEONE WITH A NET WORTH OF $1 MILLION

$

BILL GATES' NET WORTH OF $59 BILLION

$$$
$$$
$$$
$$$
$$$
$$$
$$$
$$$
$$$
$$$
$$$
$$$
$$$
$$$
$$$
$$$
$$$
$$$

$$
$$
$$
$$
$$
$$
$$
$$
$$
$$
$$
$$
$$
$$
$$
$$
$$
$$
$$
$$
$$
$$
$$

$$
$$
$$
$$
$$
$$
$$
$$
$$
$$
$$
$$
$$
$$
$$
$$
$$
$$
$$
$$
$$
$$

$$
$$
$$
$$
$$
$$
$$
$$
$$
$$
$$
$$
$$
$$
$$
$$
$$
$$
$$
$$
$$
$$

$$
$$
$$
$$
$$
$$
$$
$$
$$
$$
$$
$$
$$
$$
$$
$$
$$
$$
$$
$$
$$
$$

$$
$$
$$
$$
$$
$$
$$
$$
$$
$$
$$
$$
$$
$$
$$
$$
$$
$$
$$
$$
$$
$$
$$

$$$
$$$
$$$
$$$
$$$
$$$
$$$
$$$
$$$
$$$
$$$
$$$
$$$
$$$
$$$
$$$
$$$
$$$
$$$
$$$
$$$
$$$

$$$
$$$
$$$
$$$
$$$
$$$
$$$
$$$
$$$
$$$$$$$$$$$$$$$$$$$$$$$$$$$$$$$$$$$$$

Remember, each $ equals <u>$1 MILLION</u>.

$$$
$$$
$$$
$$$
$$$
$$$
$$$
$$$
$$$
$$$
$$$
$$$

$$$
$$$
$$$
$$$
$$$
$$$
$$$
$$$
$$$
$$$
$$$
$$$
$$$
$$$
$$$
$$$
$$$
$$$
$$$
$$$
$$$
$$$

$$
$$
$$
$$
$$
$$
$$
$$
$$
$$
$$
$$
$$
$$
$$
$$
$$
$$
$$
$$
$$
$$

$$
$$
$$
$$
$$
$$
$$
$$
$$
$$
$$
$$
$$
$$
$$
$$
$$
$$
$$
$$
$$
$$

$$$
$$$
$$$
$$$
$$$
$$$
$$$
$$$
$$$
$$$
$$$
$$$
$$$
$$$
$$$
$$$
$$$
$$$
$$$
$$$
$$$
$$$
$$$
$$$

$$
$$
$$
$$
$$
$$
$$
$$
$$
$$
$$
$$
$$
$$
$$
$$
$$
$$
$$
$$
$$
$$

$$
$$
$$
$$
$$
$$
$$
$$
$$
$$
$$
$$
$$
$$
$$
$$
$$
$$
$$
$$
$$
$$
$$

$$
$$
$$
$$
$$
$$
$$
$$
$$
$$
$$
$$
$$
$$
$$
$$
$$
$$
$$
$$
$$
$$

$$
$$
$$
$$
$$
$$
$$
$$
$$
$$
$$
$$
$$
$$
$$
$$
$$
$$
$$
$$
$$
$$
$$

$$$
$$$
$$$
$$$
$$$
$$$
$$$
$$$
$$$
$$$
$$$
$$$
$$$
$$$
$$$
$$$
$$$
$$$
$$$
$$$
$$$
$$$

$$
$$
$$
$$
$$
$$
$$
$$
$$
$$
$$
$$
$$
$$
$$
$$
$$
$$
$$
$$
$$
$$

$$$$$$$$$$$$$$$$$$$$$$$$$$$$$$$$$$$$$$
$$$$$$$$$$$$$$$$$$$$$$$$$$$$$$$$$$$$$$
$$$$$$$$$$$$$$$$$$$$$$$$$$$$$$$$$$$$$$
$$$$$$$$$$$$$$$$$$$$$$$$$$$$$$$$$$$$$$
$$$$$$$$$$$$$$$$$$$$$$$$$$$$$$$$$$$$$$
$$$$$$$$$$$$$$$$$$$$$$$$$$$$$$$$$$$$$$
$$$$$$$$$$$$$$$$$$$$$$$$$$$$$$$$$$$$$$
$$$$$$$$$$$$$$$$$$$$$$$$$$$$$$$$$$$$$$
$$$$$$$$$$$$$$$$$$$$$$$$$$$$$$$$$$$$$$
$$$$$$$$$$$$$$$$$$$$$$$$$$$$$$$$$$$$$$
$$$$$$$$$$$$$$$$$$$$$$$$$$$$$$$$$$$$$$
$$$$$$$$$$$$$$$$$$$$$$$$$$$$$$$$$$$$$$
$$$$$$$$$$$$$$$$$$$$$$$$$$$$$$$$$$$$$$
$$$$$$$$$$$$$$$$$$$$$$$$$$$$$$$$$$$$$$
$$$$$$$$$$$$$$$$$$$$$$$$$$$$$$$$$$$$$$
$$$$$$$$$$$$$$$$$$$$$$$$$$$$$$$$$$$$$$
$$$$$$$$$$$$$$$$$$$$$$$$$$$$$$$$$$$$$$
$$$$$$$$$$$$$$$$$$$$$$$$$$$$$$$$$$$$$$
$$$$$$$$$$$$$$$$$$$$$$$$$$$$$$$$$$$$$$
$$$$$$$$$$$$$$$$$$$$$$$$$$$$$$$$$$$$$$
$$$$$$$$$$$$$$$$$$$$$$$$$$$$$$$$$$$$$$
$$$$$$$$$$$$$$$$$$$$$$$$$$$$$$$$$$$$$$

$$$
$$$
$$$
$$$
$$$
$$$
$$$
$$$
$$$$$$$$$$$$$$$$$$$$$$$$$$$$$$$$$$$$$$

Believe it or not, we still have a *long* way to
go.

$$$
$$$
$$$
$$$
$$$
$$$
$$$
$$$
$$$
$$$
$$$
$$$

$$
$$
$$
$$
$$
$$
$$
$$
$$
$$
$$
$$
$$
$$
$$
$$
$$
$$
$$
$$
$$
$$

$$
$$
$$
$$
$$
$$
$$
$$
$$
$$
$$
$$
$$
$$
$$
$$
$$
$$
$$
$$
$$
$$

$$
$$
$$
$$
$$
$$
$$
$$
$$
$$
$$
$$
$$
$$
$$
$$
$$
$$
$$
$$
$$
$$

$$$
$$$
$$$
$$$
$$$
$$$
$$$
$$$
$$$
$$$
$$$
$$$
$$$
$$$
$$$
$$$
$$$
$$$
$$$
$$$
$$$
$$$

$$
$$
$$
$$
$$
$$
$$
$$
$$
$$
$$
$$
$$
$$
$$
$$
$$
$$
$$
$$
$$
$$

$$$
$$$
$$$
$$$
$$$
$$$
$$$
$$$
$$$
$$$
$$$
$$$
$$$
$$$
$$$
$$$
$$$
$$$
$$$
$$$
$$$
$$$
$$$

$$
$$
$$
$$
$$
$$
$$
$$
$$
$$
$$
$$
$$
$$
$$
$$
$$
$$
$$
$$
$$
$$

$$
$$
$$
$$
$$
$$
$$
$$
$$
$$
$$
$$
$$
$$
$$
$$
$$
$$
$$
$$
$$
$$

$$
$$
$$
$$
$$
$$
$$
$$
$$
$$
$$
$$
$$
$$
$$
$$
$$
$$
$$
$$
$$
$$

$$$
$$$
$$$
$$$
$$$
$$$
$$$
$$$
$$$
$$$
$$$
$$$
$$$
$$$
$$$
$$$
$$$
$$$
$$$
$$$
$$$
$$$

$$
$$
$$
$$
$$
$$
$$
$$
$$
$$
$$
$$
$$
$$
$$
$$
$$
$$
$$
$$
$$
$$

$$$
$$$
$$$
$$$
$$$
$$$$$$$$$$$$$$$$$$$$$$$$$$$$

Each $ equals $1 MILLION

$$$
$$$
$$$
$$$
$$$
$$$
$$$
$$$
$$$
$$$
$$$
$$$
$$$
$$$
$$$

$$
$$
$$
$$
$$
$$
$$
$$
$$
$$
$$
$$
$$
$$
$$
$$
$$
$$
$$
$$
$$
$$

$$$
$$$
$$$
$$$
$$$
$$$
$$$
$$$
$$$
$$$
$$$
$$$
$$$
$$$
$$$
$$$
$$$
$$$
$$$
$$$
$$$
$$$

$$$
$$$
$$$
$$$
$$$
$$$
$$$
$$$
$$$
$$$
$$$
$$$
$$$
$$$
$$$
$$$
$$$
$$$
$$$
$$$
$$$

$$
$$
$$
$$
$$
$$
$$
$$
$$
$$
$$
$$
$$
$$
$$
$$
$$
$$
$$
$$
$$
$$
$$

$$
$$
$$
$$
$$
$$
$$
$$
$$
$$
$$
$$
$$
$$
$$
$$
$$
$$
$$
$$
$$
$$

$$
$$
$$
$$
$$$$$$$$$$$$$

Does Bill Gates possess all the money in the world?

$$
$$
$$
$$
$$
$$
$$
$$
$$
$$
$$
$$
$$
$$
$$

$$
$$
$$
$$
$$
$$
$$
$$
$$
$$
$$
$$
$$
$$
$$
$$
$$
$$
$$
$$
$$
$$

$$
$$
$$
$$
$$
$$
$$
$$
$$
$$
$$
$$
$$
$$
$$
$$
$$
$$
$$
$$
$$
$$
$$

$$
$$
$$
$$
$$
$$
$$
$$
$$
$$
$$
$$
$$
$$
$$
$$
$$
$$
$$
$$
$$
$$

$$
$$
$$
$$
$$
$$
$$
$$
$$
$$
$$
$$
$$
$$
$$
$$
$$
$$
$$
$$
$$
$$
$$

$$$$$$$$$$$$$$$$$$$$$$$$$$$$$$$$$$$$$
$$$$$$$$$$$$$$$$$$$$$$$$$$$$$$$$$$$$$
$$$$$$$$$$$$$$$$$$$$$$$$$$$$$$$$$$$$$
$$$$$$$$$$$$$$$$$$$$$$$$$$$$$$$$$$$$$
$$$$$$$$$$$$$$$$$$$$$$$$$$$$$$$$$$$$$
$$$$$$$$$$$$$$$$$$$$$$$$$$$$$$$$$$$$$
$$$$$$$$$$$$$$$$$$$$$$$$$$$$$$$$$$$$$
$$$$$$$$$$$$$$$$$$$$$$$$$$$$$$$$$$$$$
$$$$$$$$$$$$$$$$$$$$$$$$$$$$$$$$$$$$$
$$$$$$$$$$$$$$$$$$$$$$$$$$$$$$$$$$$$$
$$$$$$$$$$$$$$$$$$$$$$$$$$$$$$$$$$$$$
$$$$$$$$$$$$$$$$$$$$$$$$$$$$$$$$$$$$$
$$$$$$$$$$$$$$$$$$$$$$$$$$$$$$$$$$$$$
$$$$$$$$$$$$$$$$$$$$$$$$$$$$$$$$$$$$$
$$$$$$$$$$$$$$$$$$$$$$$$$$$$$$$$$$$$$
$$$$$$$$$$$$$$$$$$$$$$$$$$$$$$$$$$$$$
$$$$$$$$$$$$$$$$$$$$$$$$$$$$$$$$$$$$$
$$$$$$$$$$$$$$$$$$$$$$$$$$$$$$$$$$$$$
$$$$$$$$$$$$$$$$$$$$$$$$$$$$$$$$$$$$$
$$$$$$$$$$$$$$$$$$$$$$$$$$$$$$$$$$$$$
$$$$$$$$$$$$$$$$$$$$$$$$$$$$$$$$$$$$$
$$$$$$$$$$$$$$$$$$$$$$$$$$$$$$$$$$$$$

$$
$$
$$
$$
$$
$$
$$
$$
$$
$$
$$
$$
$$
$$
$$
$$
$$
$$
$$
$$
$$
$$
$$

$$
$$
$$
$$
$$
$$
$$
$$
$$
$$
$$
$$
$$
$$
$$
$$
$$
$$
$$
$$
$$
$$

$$$
$$$
$$$
$$$
$$$
$$$
$$$
$$$
$$$
$$$
$$$
$$$
$$$
$$$
$$$
$$$
$$$
$$$
$$$
$$$
$$$
$$$
$$$

$$
$$
$$
$$
$$
$$
$$
$$
$$
$$
$$
$$
$$
$$
$$
$$
$$
$$
$$
$$
$$
$$

$$
$$
$$
$$
$$
$$
$$
$$
$$
$$
$$
$$
$$
$$
$$
$$
$$
$$
$$
$$
$$
$$

$$
$$
$$
$$
$$
$$
$$
$$
$$
$$
$$
$$
$$
$$
$$
$$
$$
$$
$$
$$
$$

$$$
$$$
$$$
$$$
$$$
$$$
$$$
$$$
$$$
$$$
$$$
$$$
$$$
$$$
$$$
$$$
$$$
$$$
$$$
$$$
$$$
$$$
$$$

$$$
$$$
$$$
$$$
$$$
$$$
$$$
$$$
$$$
$$$
$$$
$$$
$$$
$$$
$$$
$$$
$$$
$$$
$$$
$$$
$$$
$$$

$$$
$$$
$$$
$$$
$$$
$$$
$$$
$$$
$$$
$$$
$$$
$$$
$$$
$$$
$$$
$$$
$$$
$$$
$$$
$$$
$$$
$$$
$$$

$$$
$$$
$$$
$$$
$$$
$$$
$$$
$$$
$$$
$$$
$$$
$$$
$$$
$$$
$$$
$$$
$$$
$$$
$$$
$$$
$$$
$$$

$$
$$
$$
$$
$$
$$
$$
$$
$$
$$
$$
$$
$$
$$
$$
$$
$$
$$
$$
$$
$$

$$
$$
$$
$$
$$
$$
$$
$$
$$
$$
$$

Remember, our millionaire only had *one* $

$$
$$
$$
$$
$$
$$
$$
$$
$$
$$
$$

$$$
$$$
$$$
$$$
$$$
$$$
$$$
$$$
$$$
$$$
$$$
$$$
$$$
$$$
$$$
$$$
$$$
$$$
$$$
$$$
$$$
$$$
$$$

$$
$$
$$
$$
$$
$$
$$
$$
$$
$$
$$
$$
$$
$$
$$
$$
$$
$$
$$
$$
$$
$$

$$$
$$$
$$$
$$$
$$$
$$$
$$$
$$$
$$$
$$$
$$$
$$$
$$$
$$$
$$$
$$$
$$$
$$$
$$$
$$$
$$$
$$$

$$$
$$$
$$$
$$$
$$$
$$$
$$$
$$$
$$$
$$$
$$$
$$$
$$$
$$$
$$$
$$$
$$$
$$$
$$$
$$$
$$$
$$$
$$$

$$
$$
$$
$$
$$
$$
$$
$$
$$
$$
$$
$$
$$
$$
$$
$$
$$
$$
$$
$$
$$
$$
$$

$$
$$
$$
$$
$$
$$
$$
$$
$$
$$
$$
$$
$$
$$
$$
$$
$$
$$
$$
$$
$$
$$

$$
$$
$$
$$
$$
$$
$$
$$
$$
$$
$$
$$
$$
$$
$$
$$
$$
$$
$$
$$
$$
$$

$$$
$$$
$$$
$$$
$$$
$$$
$$$
$$$
$$$
$$$
$$$
$$$
$$$
$$$
$$$
$$$
$$$
$$$
$$$
$$$
$$$
$$$
$$$
$$$

$$
$$
$$
$$
$$
$$
$$
$$
$$
$$
$$
$$
$$
$$
$$
$$
$$
$$
$$
$$
$$
$$
$$
$$

$$$
$$$
$$$
$$$
$$$
$$$
$$$
$$$
$$$
$$$
$$$
$$$
$$$
$$$
$$$
$$$
$$$
$$$
$$$
$$$
$$$
$$$

$$$
$$
$$
$$
$$
$$
$$
$$
$$
$$
$$
$$
$$
$$
$$
$$
$$
$$
$$
$$
$$
$$

$$$
$$$
$$$
$$$
$$$
$$$
$$$
$$$
$$$
$$$
$$$
$$$
$$$
$$$
$$$
$$$
$$$
$$$
$$$
$$$
$$$

$$$
$$$
$$$
$$$
$$$
$$$
$$$
$$$
$$$
$$$
$$$
$$$
$$$
$$$
$$$
$$$
$$$
$$$
$$$
$$$
$$$
$$$
$$$
$$$
$$$

$$$
$$$
$$$
$$$
$$$
$$$
$$$
$$$
$$$
$$$
$$$
$$$
$$$
$$$
$$$
$$$
$$$
$$$
$$$
$$$
$$$
$$$

$$
$$
$$
$$
$$
$$
$$
$$
$$
$$
$$
$$
$$
$$
$$
$$
$$
$$
$$$$$$$$$$$$$$$$$$$$$$$$$$$$$$$$$$$$$$

Believe it or not, Bill Gates is $59,000$ times richer than someone with a net worth of one million dollars.

PART B:

THAT'S ENTERTAINMENT!

This part of the book is to be taken not as fact but purely for entertainment purposes.

Any resemblance within this section to any billionaire living, dead, or pretending to reside in Monaco or Dubai in order to avoid paying taxes is purely coincidental.

AT THE MOVIES WITH STEVE FARBES

REVIEW OF

IT'S A WONDERFUL LIFE

The plot of *It's a Wonderful Life* revolves around a two-bit liberal huckster by the name of George Bailey. Soon after the movie begins, we learn that this George Bailey is a restless hobo-wannabe whose one constant thought is to abandon his family, friends, and hometown so that he can pursue a life of adventure and self-gratification in far-off lands. We first see the grown up George in a store in Bedford Falls where he receives a free suitcase courtesy of the town drug dealer, a Mr. Gower. The socialist George Bailey unabashedly accepts the undeserved gift, reflecting his lifelong liberal philosophy of receiving something for nothing. We also see evidence of his lazy liberal attitude in his often-repeated wish (made on some cheap soda shop contraption) to be given rather than work for a million dollars.

We get another glimpse of George Bailey's exceedingly self-serving attitude early in the story when his frail and over-worked father begs him to consider working at the savings and loan after he attends college. George immediately refuses to even consider helping his father, saying he would rather build bridges in Bangladesh or skyscrapers in Samarkand. After callously dashing his father's dreams of retirement, the pleasure-seeking George selfishly heads off to the town high school to attend a wild dance party. It is here that he hooks up with a raven-haired temptress by the name of Mary. These two lecherous liberals proceed to shamelessly shake their asses to riotous boogie-woogie music in front of the frenzied and gawking high school student body before receiving their just desserts by plunging head first into a below-floor swimming pool.

George then escorts the scantily-clad Mary home. During their walk through town, they commit an act of vandalism by inexplicably shattering panes of glass in a charming old Victorian house. While his father lies dying of exhaustion and a broken heart, George shamelessly continues to court the under-age Mary during their criminal jaunt through the dark back roads of Bedford Falls. At one point, George's need for instant sexual gratification overcomes him as he rips off the unsuspecting young lady's terry cloth robe. Mary, completely nude at this point, plunges into a nearby hydrangea bush in an attempt to conceal herself from the violent sexual predator. Revealing the base nature of his character, George refuses to return the robe to her as he derives the greatest pleasure from taunting the young tramp due to her desperate predicament. She is only saved from being raped by George by a passing motorist who informs him that his decision not to work at the savings and loan has killed his father.

It is at this point in the story that a Mr. Potter makes his appearance. His character is the one redeeming element amongst all of the other bums and socialist rabble in the movie. If one were desirous to find a businessman upon whom one should model oneself, Mr. Potter would be the person. Crafty, astute, and undeterred by the useless emotions of compassion and sympathy, Mr. Potter wisely and with good-old American industry and gumption continually acquires under his benevolent control more and more of the poorly-run businesses in Bedford Falls, ushering in minimum-wage jobs, gin joints, and whore houses for the grateful masses. The only person standing in the way of his complete domination of the town is the singularly unlikeable and despicable schemer, George Bailey, whose greatest desire is to bring socialism to his hometown.

It is in the scene just after George Bailey murders his father that the socialist, George, and the free-market advocate, Mr. Potter, square off. Here, we find the prim and dapper Mr. Potter attempting to reason with the weak-minded board of directors of the savings and loan. With impeccable logic and business sense, he tells them that the poorly-managed bank should be immediately dissolved due to the untimely demise of George's father. It is at this point that the irate and irrational George goes off on a rant, threatening the defenseless, wheelchair-bound Mr. Potter. Mr. Potter, out of respect for the death of the young maniac's father, patiently listens to the senseless and emotional tirade by the liberal thug, George Bailey. After George's emotional, bleeding-heart liberal outburst, the irrational and mindless board decides not to dissolve the bank, but only under the condition that George take over as manager. George, the consummate bum who doesn't want to work for a living but rather live off handouts from the state, is compelled to take on responsibility for the first time in his life, dashing his dreams of gallivanting around the globe in pursuit of cheap thrills and loose women.

With no other choice but to remain in his hometown, George, ever the unsatisfied and restless idler, settles down despite himself and marries the hot-to-trot Mary. On their wedding day, as fate would have it, a bank run takes place at his savings and loan. The townspeople, finally wising up to George's socialistic, liberal-do-gooder business practices, become fearful that their hard-earned deposits may not be safe in George's communist-style bank. Fortunately, Mr. Potter, out of the kindness of his heart, generously offers fifty cents on the dollar to all of the desperate depositors at George's mismanaged savings and loan; George, however, hypnotizes the mindless hoard by brandishing a thick wad of money and cajoling them with some lame cock and bull stories about Mr. Potter being some kind of opportunist devil.

One would think that after all of the slanderous accusations George Bailey had made about him, Mr. Potter would be embittered, but this is not the case. Despite all of the malicious aspersions cast by George towards the crippled old gent, Mr. Potter, in Christ-like fashion, offers the undeserving George a job in his prosperous company. George is initially tempted by the high-paying position, but then quickly realizes that accepting the job would entail actually doing some hard work; he therefore turns down

241

Mr. Potter's extremely generous offer by violently yelling and screaming at him and also at his stunned and slack-jawed assistant.

Later in the story, an auditor arrives at the savings and loan to see how George and his fellow socialist crooks have cooked the books. Even while the determined auditor is examining the bank's accounts payable and receivable just feet away, George Bailey shamelessly escorts a blonde hussy into his private office in the hopes of seducing her. He attempts to entice the wayward blonde by giving her a large chunk of the bank's money. This dirty money is intended to allow the coquettish harlot to satisfy her wish to leave Bedford Falls and head to the big city for a life of wanton debauchery. In the end, George, a married man dizzy with desire for the town pump, emerges from his office with a lipstick-covered face from the make-out session with the dizzy blonde.

At the same time that this indecency is taking place, one of the employees of the poorly-managed savings and loan, an absent-minded old numbskull by the name of Uncle Billy, carelessly places the bank's daily proceeds inside Mr. Potter's newspaper. Mr. Potter, having been viciously mocked by the cackling and gloating Uncle Billy, is initially unaware of the transfer of funds from the elderly and brainless kook standing before him. Upon discovering the substantial sum of money now in his possession, he does not return it to the blathering fool –although this is his greatest desire- but instead has his trusty assistant sequester him away to his private office. Although in his heart he earnestly wishes to return the money to Uncle Billy, he immediately realizes that the humane thing to do is to keep the money so that the old fool will learn to be more diligent henceforth with all of his business endeavors. As such, Mr. Potter wisely realizes that the long-term benefits of increased vigilance and professionalism will far outweigh the short-term hardship.

After Uncle Billy returns to the bank and informs George of the mysterious loss of the bank's money, George Bailey throws a lifetime of friendship down the drain by violently screaming at the enfeebled Uncle Billy, telling the old loser that one of them is going to jail, thereby reducing the poor old fool to tears. George, the consummate coward that he is, informs the now blathering Uncle Billy that he will let him solely take the rap.

George Bailey, finally paying the price for years and years of indulgent managerial practices, like a coward, runs home to his family to hide out from the authorities. It is here that the full extent of his ignorance – shown by his inability to spell the word "Frankenstein" – and his meanness – displayed by his ill treatment of his loving family- is made readily apparent. At one point he mercilessly torments his young daughter by first demanding that she stop playing a charming rendition of "Jingle Bells" and then moments later, in typical wishy-washy liberal fashion, insists that she play the selfsame song. Angered by his daughter's pathetic tears and the horrified looks from the rest of his family, the socialist, George Bailey, storms out of the house into the chill December night in pursuit of a stiff drink.

After getting socked in the jaw at the local bar, George Bailey, a confirmed alcoholic and hater of all school teachers, wisely decides to kill himself by jumping off a bridge. Unfortunately, before he is able to carry out his intention, a stupid, unwinged, second-class angel named Clarence jumps into the freezing water below, prompting the bleeding-heart liberal do-gooder, George Bailey, to jump in and save him. After extracting the useless angel from the icy water, George astutely tells the moronic angel that his life has been a complete waste of time, that the world would have been a better place if he had never been born. Rather than telling George that he has correctly summed up his life, the stupid angel shows him what the world would have been like if he'd never existed. What follows is a lot of sentimental drivel about not saving his brother's life, keeping his mother from becoming a penniless old crone, and being unable to provide decent homes to a bunch of garlic eaters.

After awakening from his "dream", we find George talking to himself on a snow-covered bridge. Ecstatic to be alive, he runs through the center of Bedford Falls while yelling and screaming like an escaped mental patient. During his frenetic gallop through town, he yells "Merry Christmas!" at inanimate objects such as the local emporium and savings and loan, perversely rejoices at the fact that he's going to jail, and tells his frightened children that he wants to eat them.

In the end, the communist parasite, George Bailey, freeloads off of the entire town. His irrational wife (who incidentally, at one point in the drama, inexplicably destroys a perfectly fine record in a fit of unrestrained anger when George Bailey refuses to make violent love to her) coerces most of the citizens of Bedford Falls to bail out her fugitive husband. This scene shows that under a liberal economic system, taxes wrenched from the hard-working citizens of the community will inevitably be used to support the ungrateful socialist slackers. Under George's fairy-tale economic system, not only is financial irresponsibility praised and encouraged, but a resultant breakdown of the law will be sure to follow, shown by the tearing up of the warrant for George's arrest. In typical socialist fashion, the story ends with George Bailey accepting the baskets of undeserved loot rather than going to the one place he rightly belongs: prison.

Rating: $

Rating Key

$$$$ = Excellent

$$$ = Good

$$ = Fair

$ = Obvious vehicle for socialist ideology

The balcony is closed to all but those select few members of the Great American Plutocracy

A DAY IN THE LIFE

OF

Christy Walton & Christy Bligh

CHRISTY WALTON

WALMART CO-OWNER

NET WORTH: $24.5 BILLION

CHRISTY BLIGH

WALMART GREETER

NET WORTH: $0.00

6:30 A.M.

CHRISTY WALTON

Blissfully sleeps in four-poster mahogany bed formerly owned by Napoleon Bonaparte.

CHRISTY BLIGH

Awakens to the sound of a monstrous belch from neighbor's studio apartment.

8:00 A.M.

CHRISTY WALTON

Informs house staff through bedroom intercom that she shall breakfast on the south veranda this morning.

CHRISTY BLIGH

Heads to work in 1984 Ford Escort.

8:30 A.M.

CHRISTY WALTON

Spends the next hour-and-a-half learning the delicate intricacies of a Japanese tea ceremony from a Zen Master.

CHRISTY BLIGH

Arrives at work. Reluctantly takes part in demeaning morning pep rally. Balled out by acne-faced manager for not displaying enough glee.

10:00 A.M.

CHRISTY WALTON

Fires entire cleaning staff when a single Cheerio is discovered underneath the refrigerator.

CHRISTY BLIGH

Pretends to happily say goodbye to departing customers while clandestinely appraising them for suspicious, thief-like behavior.

NOON

CHRISTY WALTON

Flies to Paris in private jet.

CHRISTY BLIGH

Eats brown-bagged bologna sandwich and black-spotted banana in dumpy employee lounge.

5:00 P.M.

CHRISTY WALTON

At 36,000 feet over the Atlantic Ocean, calls V.P. of Operations in China to inquire if the workforce could be "encouraged" to increase productivity by 15%.

CHRISTY BLIGH

Clocks out. During drive home, shifting mechanism falls through floor of car. Walks remaining three miles to apartment complex.

8:00 P.M.

CHRISTY WALTON

Arrives in Paris. Takes a moon-lit stroll along the Seine.

CHRISTY BLIGH

Settles down for a night of T.V. entertainment. Rescans converter box twelve times in a desperate attempt to bring in *Barney Miller*.

10:00 P.M.

CHRISTY WALTON

Partakes of a libation on the balcony of the Ritz Carlton Presidential Suite. Detects the heavenly sent of hyacinth and lavender wafting on the gentle summer breeze.

CHRISTY BLIGH

Downs six Coors and staggers towards her fold-out bed. Passes out before reaching her target.

THE PLUTOCRAT PRESS

SPECIAL EDITION

MARCH 15, 2011

"WHAT IS TO BE DONE?"

As we freedom-loving Americans are all painfully aware, current economic conditions have deteriorated to such an extent that the certainty of our economic hegemony in the world has become questionable. The combined effect of unwise and unethical regulations imposed on business – Wall Street, the banking industry and the oil companies being prime examples – and massive entitlements to the greedy working class have led us down the path to financial ruin. We are certain that we can all agree, both level-headed capitalists and wishy-washy liberal do-gooders, that if something isn't done immediately to address the problem, we may soon find ourselves in the grip of an economic depression.

Fortunately, we at the *Plutocrat Press* are not the type of people who will apathetically sit back while our beloved country crumbles to the ground. This is a time for decisive action not wimpy liberal apathy and resignation. As such, we at the *Plutocrat Press* have taken it upon ourselves to devise a pragmatic solution to our current economic crisis. After extensive consideration and heated debate among the learned members of our august body, we believe that we have found a solution that will ensure the United States' position at the forefront of economic prosperity. The conclusion at which we have arrived, although perhaps not to the liking of every segment of our great society, will, we believe, be determined to be the most practical solution to our current economic predicament. We call this plan, "*A Modest Proposal*".

A MODEST PROPOSAL

As we see it, the foremost component of our current economic system that is sucking the life out of our limited financial resources is the Soviet-style entitlement programs that exit in these United States; in particular, we are referring to the Social Security system that allows our senior citizens to receive a substantial paycheck without having to put in an honest day's work. It is astonishing that such a blatantly socialistic scheme could have ever taken root in the pure and hallowed ground of our beloved country. It goes without saying that this affront to free-market economics and the Protestant work ethic must not be allowed to continue any longer.

We at the *Plutocrat Press* have arrived at the conclusion that the only way that we can save our great country from plunging ever deeper into an economic abyss is to prevent senior citizens from receiving something for nothing. The best solution that we can think of to effect this proposition is this: on the day that an American citizen reaches retirement age – which, incidentally, we believe should be moved to age 72 – and is not able or willing to support himself without receiving a handout from the government, he should willingly take his own life. If he is resistant to the idea of killing himself, then the state would be compelled to end it for him by force. Although this may seem to be an extreme measure by some, it is the opinion of the members of the *Plutocrat Press* that it is simply the right thing to do.

Of course, it goes without saying that those retirees among us who possess sufficient means to remain financially independent - for example billionaires - would be exempt from the requirement of committing suicide; as such, they would be allowed to live out their lives in the lap of luxury and comfort which they so rightly deserve.

For those financially dependent retirees who are willing to perform their patriotic duty by kindly dying, but require a gentle, loving nudge towards death, services will be provided to aid them in their valiant obligation. We at the *Plutocrat Press* envision what would be known as "*Patriot Death Centers*" (PDC's) located across the country. These humane, for-profit death centers will be conveniently located within easy driving distance of all of our Elder Statesmen. If, for any reason, the retiree is unable to get to the PDC, transportation will be provided free of charge. (The for-profit PDC will, of course, be compensated for the cost of transportation at twenty-five and one-half times the going taxi cab rate, plus applicable gratuity. In addition, construction and operation of the PDC nationwide system will be awarded by a no-bid contract to the Halliburton Corporation.)

Rest assured that the PDC's will be run with the utmost degree of humanity and professionalism; for example, upon arrival at one of the death centers, the Elder Statesman will receive a firm handshake and a proper military salute as a display of the country's gratitude and appreciation for his decision to end his now purposeless and unproductive life; then, the Elder Statesman and the attending military officer will recite the Pledge of Allegiance; after this, the Elder Statesman will be offered a competitively-priced last meal and will then be escorted to the Death Chamber, hereafter referred to as the "*Chamber of Heroes*", whereupon, a spry nurse will clandestinely approach him from behind and inject him with a deadly poison.

We realize that things most likely will not proceed as smoothly as we would like; there are bound to be those selfish individuals who will wish to continue their unproductive lives at the expense of their country. These traitors (no other word more aptly describes them) will need to be dealt with in the severest manner possible. As such, a specialized, highly-trained Death Squad, hereafter referred to as the "*Defenders of Freedom*", will be dedicated to the patriotic task of tracking down and viciously murdering those retirees who will not willingly die.

This proposal, if faithfully carried out, would free up an enormous amount of money that otherwise would be wasted on worthless retirees. Instead of giving a handout to the undeserving masses, we could give a handout to the productive super-rich in the form of Wall Street bailouts, the elimination of capital gains taxes, and the massive expansion of publically funded, privately owned and operated mega prisons across this great and gloriously punitive land of ours.

God bless capitalism and

God bless the United States of America!

THE THREE PENNY OPERA

AIN'T WE GOT FUNDS

In depression, in recession, ain't we got funds?

Country's losing money, oh, but honey

Ain't we got funds?

The masses are starving

They're trembling with fear

But our net worth's rising

Growing fatter every year.

In the city, in the country

Ain't we got funds?

Poor kids are crying, bums are dying

Ain't we got funds?

If wifey wishes to live in Bel Aire

I'll buy her a mansion

The fifth I've bought this year.

The poor are mad and getting madder

Ain't we got funds?

Times are bad and getting badder

Still we've got funds

If things get worse, dear,

they'll go on attack

But until that time, dear,

they can all just kiss my ass

In depression, in recession

Ain't we got funds!

"From each, at a decreasing rate as net worth increases.

To each, at an increasing rate as net worth increases."

-Capitalist reworking of Marx's

famous proposition in the

Communist Manifesto.

THE DEVIL'S DICTIONARY

PLUTOCRACY \Noun [Greek: ploutokratia, contraction: plouto – thief and kratia – government, lit., those who steal with impunity with the aid of the government. 1) A government controlled by the wealthy. 2) political system of the rich, by the rich, and for the rich. 3) a country's true controlling class, as opposed to the sniveling poor. The word plutocracy describes a government which is controlled by the wealthy. As a rule, the rich overlords skillfully manage to trick the lowly masses into believing that they are living in a Democracy in which power rests in the hands of the average voter. This is accomplished by means of buying and controlling all of the major media outlets – TV, radio, newspapers – so that they can readily brainwash the masses like a bleach-filled washing machine whitens a tube sock.

Usage

-The financier's plutocratic philosophy pleased the Devil.

-The billionaire plutocrat hired the assassin to "silence" the meddlesome liberal agitator.

-I screwed my country plutocratically.

-The secretive gathering of plutocrats decided who would be "elected" President of the United States next year.

Synonyms: Fascism; U.S. Government.

WHO WANTS TO BE A BILLIONAIRE?

Int. Studio / Night

Enter Regis Hasbin and Oprah Winfrey.

REGIS HASBIN

Welcome to *Who Wants to Be a Billionaire?* On today's show, we are very privileged to have the one, the only Oprah Winfrey. Thank you for taking time out of your busy schedule to be with us.

OPRAH

You're more than welcome, Regis. I truly believe that I was put on this planet to make people happy and to give, give, give.

REGIS

You are truly a saint and an inspiration to millions, no billions of mindless buffoons around the world.

OPRAH

I couldn't agree more, Regis.

Riotous applause erupts from the studio audience lasting for twenty minutes. It only ceases when Oprah raises her hand, resulting in immediate silence.

REGIS

Shall we begin?

OPRAH

Please do.

REGIS

Alright. In 2005 Hurricane Katrina hit the southern coast of the United States, causing an estimated $125 billion in damages. How much of your massive personal wealth did you donate to help the desperate victims of the disaster?

A) $1 billion
B) $100 million
C) $10 million
D) All of my money was tied up in cash.

OPRAH

Well, I can't be certain of course. You'd have to ask one of my accountants. But I believe the answer is D, all of my money was tied up in cash.

REGIS

That is correct! You've just won $1 million. Would you like to continue?

OPRAH

I may as well, Regis. I certainly can't do much with a measly $1 million.

The boneheaded audience chuckles and nods their heads in agreement.

REGIS

Very true. And now, here is your next question. From June 2007 to June 2008, you made an estimated $275 million, which works out to approximately $753,000 per day. Meanwhile, the unemployment rate among African Americans rose to 15%. In that year, how many shows did you devote to the desperate plight of the poor who were unable to find jobs?

A) Ten shows

B) Eight shows
C) Five shows
D) Not one because appearances by Tom Cruise and
   John Travolta were more important.

OPRAH

Well, the abject poverty of the sniveling poor may very
well be unfortunate, but Tom Cruise wind surfing on a
couch or John Travolta explaining that he does several
hundred crunches daily to maintain his washboard stomach
has an entertainment value that simply cannot be matched
by depressing poor people.

REGIS

I'd rather see Tom Cruise riding a couch than a bum in an
unemployment line any day of the week. Don't you agree
audience?

*The unjustifiably giddy audience explodes with
cacophonous applause. Suddenly, Oprah interjects in a
prolonged, bellowing ejaculation:*

OPRAH

JOHN TRAVOLTAAAAAAAAAAAAAAA!!!

*The audience is unable to contain its unbounded excitement
at Oprah's obnoxious utterance. After a seemingly
interminable period of time, Oprah must suppress the
riotous cheers and applause by raising her right hand in a
fashion reminiscent of the Pope quieting the multitudes at
Saint Peter's Basilica.*

REGIS

Oprah Winfrey, you've just won $100 million!

OPRAH

That's wonderful, Regis. I can do so much good with that amount of money, but until I can decide how best to distribute it, I'll use it to purchase a painting by Matisse that would look absolutely charming in one of my 9 luxurious bathrooms.

REGIS

I can only hope to one day be in one of your lovely mansions and need to use the facilities. In any event, would you like to risk $100 million and try for the grand prize of $1 billion?

Oprah turns towards the spellbound audience.

OPRAH

What do you think, audience? Should I go on?

The audience, honored that she would deign to ask them what to do, screams out their desire for her to continue.

OPRAH

Regis, I must follow the will of the people. Let us continue.

REGIS

Excellent. Here is the $1 billion question: It has been said incessantly that there has never been anyone on daytime television like you, but this "greatness" of yours has actually improved the lives of how many people:

A) Every single person on the face of the planet.
B) The millions of faithful fans who religiously watch your show every day
C) The handful of people who are directly involved in the production of the extremely lucrative show.
D) Only you and Gale.

OPRAH

Well, Regis, you know that my desire to give knows no bounds, but one thing I know for certain is that I have become fabulously rich from this show, and my parasitic friend, Gale, has profited handsomely, too; therefore, I'm going to say D, Only Gale and I.

REGIS

That is correct! Despite the unrelenting propaganda campaign that brainwashed the masses into believing that they were in some way benefiting while you became unbelievably wealthy, you and Gale are the only ones who can demonstrably be shown to have benefitted. Oprah, you've just won $1 billion!

The audience explodes into riotous applause at the fact that Oprah has becoming even richer while they remain as poor as when the show began.

REGIS

Oprah, what are you going to do now?

OPRAH

The same as I've always done, Regis: Give, give, give. Well, maybe not immediately, but in the near future, perhaps, I will use this money to improve the life of every single person on the face of the planet earth.

Regis and the audience, overwhelmed by Oprah's hypothetical generosity, are reduced to blubbering idiots.

FADE OUT

DEEP THOUGHTS

If you give a man a fish, he'll eat for a day. If you don't give a man a fish, you'll save $9.95, and he'll eventually starve to death, thereby reducing the surplus population.

This is a good thing.

-The Capitalist Compendium

of Maxims, Proverbs, and

Arcane Wisdom

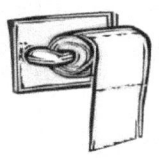

THE GREED STREET JOURNAL

AN INTERVIEW WITH

DR. MALTON FRAUDMAN

CHAIR OF THE ECONOMICS DEPARTMENT

IN THE FREEDOM GRADUATE SCHOOL

OF FREEMARKET ECONOMICS

AT PATRIOT UNIVERSITY

INTERVIEWED BY

STEVE FARBES

Steve Farbes

Thank you Dr. Fraudman for allotting us a slice of your precious time in your busy schedule.

Dr. Fraudman

It is my pleasure.

Steve Farbes

Dr. Fraudman, as you are aware, the United States is
experiencing one of the worst economic crises in its
history. Unemployment is on the rise, the cost of living is
increasing, and banks are becoming more and more
reluctant to extend loans to businesses out of fear of their
inability to repay them. In government, there is a
seemingly insurmountable gulf between the aisles as to the
cause of our present economic predicament and its requisite
cure. In your opinion, what is the greatest impediment to
America's recovery and what are the feasible solutions?

Dr. Fraudman

Without question, the greatest impediment to the present
and future prosperity of the United States is the inequitable
distribution of wealth between the rich and the middle
class/poor.

Steve Farbes

You think that the super-rich are in possession of an
excessive proportion of the United States' wealth?

Dr. Fraudman

Heavens no. Quite the opposite. It seems to me, and it is
borne out by empirical studies conducted at the *Rupert
Murdick Institute for Free Markets and Democracy*, that
the middle class and poor possess an absurdly bloated slice
of America's economic pie.

Steve Farbes

That's a very interesting perspective. Please elaborate.

Dr. Fraudman

With pleasure. As I stated earlier, the poor and middle classes possess too much and the super-rich possess too little. At the present time, the top 1% of our country possess a measly 37% of the nation's net wealth, while the remaining 99% possess a bloated 63% or almost TWO TIMES the amount possessed by the so-called super-rich. This is inherently unfair. It is not only unfair but also unethical, unscrupulous, and devastating to the present and future prosperity of our great country.

Steve Farbes

That is an absolutely fascinating position, Dr. Fraudman. Please continue if you will.

Dr. Fraudman

Gladly. As I proved through my exhaustive studies funded by a grant from the non-partisan group *Americans for a Greedier Tomorrow*, the super-rich and not the middle class or poor are the true drivers of the economy. All great innovations and advancements that spearhead the economy into ever greater productivity and prosperity are initiated, or more precisely, funded by the wealthiest members of our society. Rare is it that a member of the lowly and slow-witted proletariat, to borrow a Soviet-era term, will provide any sort of stimulus to kindle economic innovation and progress.

Steve Farbes

Fascinating. I have never thought of it in those terms, but your logic is of course flawless.

Dr. Fraudmam

Very true.

Steve Farbes

In light of this indisputable evidence, what do you propose should be done?

Dr. Fraudman

I believe that the solution to our present and future problems is to allocate wealth based on a group's abilities, not on need. As such, the super-rich, being superior in every conceivable way, should be given 75% of the nation's wealth, and the other 99% of the population, being unimaginably stupid and lazy, should be given a very generous 25% of the nation's economic pie. By wresting the stagnant and unproductive excess wealth from the greedy hands of the obtuse middle class and poor and placing it into the dynamic coffers of the economic elite, we would see a leap forward in economic productivity and consequent prosperity that has never been witnessed in the history of our great country.

Steve Farbes

This makes a great deal of sense, but do you think that 25% is the appropriate percentage of wealth to allot to the sniveling masses?

Dr. Fraudman

This is a fair question, and one that is open to a great deal of debate. I, in fact, have lain awake in bed at night and questioned if this is a fair and just distribution of the great wealth of our great country. After much thought and many additional lost hairs from my head, I have indeed determined that it is, for the time being, the most logical and equitable distribution. If, in some future point in time, it is quantitatively determined that the 75%/25% split is in fact unfair, we could always increase the super-rich's share to, say, 85% of the nation's wealth and reduce the slobbering masses' share to a more appropriate 15%.

Steve Farbes

This may be a silly question, but do you think that it would be best to place 100% of the wealth of our great nation into the industrious hands of the super-rich?

Dr. Fraudman

This idea is in no way, shape, or form silly, but rather an idea that should be seriously considered. If all of the wealth of our country - the greatest country in the history of civilization - were to be placed under the control of the super-rich, we would then have what I would call a "Dictatorship of the Rich". This, of course, would be a highly desirable state for our country to be in, and could quite possibly be the best solution to the economic woes that now confront us.

Steve Farbes

But without any net worth whatsoever, how would the other 99% of the country survive?

Dr. Fraudman

Very simply. Every family would be provided with a very small single-room hovel in which to live and an adequate allowance with which they most likely would be able to subsist, assuming, of course, that they perform the work demanded of them by their plutocratic overlords. This situation is akin to that of a parent and small child: if the child does all of his chores and shows complete subservience towards the parent, then he or she is provided with food and shelter and perhaps some spending money to purchase extravagances such as salt-water toffee or gum drops. This, of course, depends on the child showing sufficient gratitude towards the parent, or in this case the super-rich taskmaster.

Steve Farbes

Very well said, Dr. Fraudman. This has been a most enlightening discussion. Hopefully, America's political leaders will take heed of your sage advice.

Dr. Fraudman

One can only hope, Steve.

CONGRATULATIONS!

THE GREED HALL OF FAME'S ANNUAL AWARDS
CEREMONY

BEING HELD ON THE SUPER-SECRETIVE
GROUNDS OF BOHEMIA MEADOWS

PROUDLY PRESENTS THIS YEAR'S LIFETIME
ACHIEVEMENT AWARD TO

CHRISTOPHER COLUMBUS

Whose unceasing efforts to mercilessly exploit the indigenous people of the Caribbean for his own personal enrichment and glory and that of King Ferdinand and Queen Isabella of Spain led to the opening of a new and previously un-raped region of the world. Christopher Columbus's relentless pursuit of profit regardless of the misery and murder that he left in his wake has inspired countless capitalists to follow his exemplary example of placing profits before people and money before morals. Although he is responsible for the almost complete eradication of an entire race of people, his opening of a market of inestimable natural wealth far outweighs the enslavement and ultimate demise of a bunch of non-Christian savages.

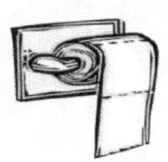

THE GREED STREET JOURNAL

"GREED, BY THE NUMBERS"

An article appearing in this month's issue of *"Mathematicians for a More Crooked Tomorrow"* has been causing quite a stir among America's economists. The article, authored by Dr. Snively Fauxvrai, asserts that he has unequivocally proven by means of an ingenious mathematical equation that greed and democracy are inextricably correlated. Dr. Fauxvrai's equation, stunning both in its simplicity and power, is presented here:

$$\underline{G = FU^{\underline{2}}}$$

Where:

G = Greed

F = Freedom

U = Utility

Dr. Fauxvrai says he has always known in his heart that greed is an indispensable component of a free society, but up until now, he has been unable to prove it. "It has been my fondest wish for many years to prove to the naysayers that having the desire and opportunity to screw your trusting neighbor out of his last hard-earned dollar in order to increase one's own financial standing is a necessary component of any free and just society."

The reaction to Dr. Fauxvrai's revolutionary equation has been mixed. The overly emotional and illogical liberals have foolishly rejected it; however, among the rational and level-headed American aristocracy, there is unanimous jubilation that the centuries' old hatred towards the economic elite has been proven untenable. "What the poor people don't understand is that when a multinational corporation fires 15,000 employees two weeks before Christmas so that the CEO can maximize the value of his stock options, the embattled CEO is actually fighting selflessly to maintain our democracy" says Dr. Fauxvrai. He further asserts that "Although it may be unfortunate that so many people can so suddenly become impoverished, they should take comfort in the fact that their misery and hopelessness and the accompanying greed of their super rich CEO are the very things that maintain the wonderful democracy in which we live."

THE DEVIL'S DICTIONARY

GREED IS GOOD: A phrase that states that the relentless pursuit of profit despite the ethical or moral impediments that may have to be hurtled is something that is advantageous to the economy as a whole. It is a concept that is specifically applied to criminal organizations - such as the Mafia, Wall Street, or the petroleum industry - to justify their immoral and illegal business activities. The phrase is specifically applied to multinational corporations and the super-rich in order to keep the masses from fomenting a revolution. As a rule, the phrase is never applied to the average worker in America - such as school teachers who ask for a two percent pay raise. With groups such as teachers and other working-class stiffs, the word "greed" is applied without the "is good" part.

Analogous Phrases

-Robbing your neighbor is good.

-Extortion is good.

-A lack of ethical business dealings is good.

"There is no greater disaster than greed."

-Lao-tzu

"You can be greedy and still feel good about yourself."

-Ivan Boesky, channeling

the thoughts of his Dark

Master, the Devil.

A DAY IN THE LIFE

OF

Michael Bloomberg & a NYC Garbageman

12:01 A.M.

MICHAEL BLOOMBERG

Since midnight, has already made

$537 while he sleeps.

NEW YORK CITY GARBAGEMAN

Begins shift. Monstrous garbage truck thunders down street at 45 mph as frightened garbageman holds on for dear life on a ridiculously narrow step.

1:30 A.M.

MICHAEL BLOOMBERG

Dreams of being a billionaire. Wakes up and realizes he already is a billionaire.

NEW YORK CITY GARBAGEMAN

Unknowingly loads a Hefty bag full of human body parts into the back of the truck. Can't find a rag to wipe unidentifiable goo off of hands.

3:00 A.M.

MICHAEL BLOOMBERG

Dreams of beautiful butterflies and happy little hummingbirds.

NEW YORK CITY GARBAGEMAN

Mugged and robbed for his plastic Homer Simpson wristwatch by street punks while attempting to load 150-pound orange carpet into truck's trash compactor.

5:00 A.M.

MICHAEL BLOOMBERG

Awakens. Places $60,000 Rolex watch on his wrist.

NEW YORK CITY GARBAGEMAN

Hands are frozen; can't feel fingertips. Wraps hands around hot tailpipe while stopped at red light.

7:00 A.M.

MICHAEL BLOOMBERG

Recites poem to himself while gazing out of floor-to-ceiling windows on a beautiful winter landscape: "God's in his heaven. All's right with the world".

NEW YORK CITY GARBAGEMAN

Ends shift covered in piss, crap, and slop.

7:30 A.M.

MICHAEL BLOOMBERG

Takes subway to Mayor's office to rule on high.

NEW YORK CITY GARBAGEMAN

Takes subway back to the ghetto. Smiles at Mayor
Bloomberg sitting across the aisle.

Greed, the final frontier

These are the voyagers of the economic
system

"Free" Enterprise

Its five year mission:

To exploit strange new worlds

To enslave new lives and new civilizations

To boldly plunder where no one has
plundered before!

THE PLUTOCRAT PRESS

May 10, 2011

AMERICAN ARISTOCRACY

VS.

THE INTERNAL REVENUE SERVICE

In a landmark case being heard before the United States Supreme Court, arguments are being presented by a consortium of 400 plutocrats. In their lawsuit, the litigants are asserting that the current tax system that is in force in regards to them is inherently unfair. The Plaintiff's side is being represented by the prestigious law firm of *We, Screw 'Em, and How*. The case being presented is comprised of numerous components, a portion of which is presented below.

Part A: We, America's richest and most pampered individuals, assert that the current graduated tax scheme represents nothing less than discrimination against those of us who happen to be members of the American Plutocracy. We Aristocrats represent a minority group no different from other minority groups - such as the niggers, spics, wops and kikes - and as such we should be afforded protection from unfair discrimination. The United States Aristocracy represents a mere 400 vulnerable individuals, far smaller than any other minority group in America, and yet it has not been provided with assistance in any way. Instead these plutocrats have been shackled by a repressive and unjust tax scheme. Every other minority group in this country has been afforded every opportunity to prosper and succeed and has been protected from unjust treatment to protect their interests. Sadly, this has not been the case with the poor American billionaire. In striking contrast to these other favored groups, he has been compelled to forge his way through life completely alone and with no protection from the government. Instead of protection, a heavy yoke of repressive taxes has been tightly placed around the tender and innocent neck of the meek and vulnerable billionaire.   It seems obvious that this unfair and unjust discrimination against America's smallest and as such most vulnerable minority group must end, but we think that it must go much further. Not only must punitive taxes on America's privileged class be abolished, but past transgressions must also be rectified. This should be accomplished by two measures:

1) An affirmative action program for billionaires should be created. This program would allow over-burdened billionaires to, for example, obtain interest-free, government-sponsored loans from banks, or better yet grants directly from the government to allow the American billionaire to get back on his feet after unending decades of hardship.

2) Reparations should be awarded to each and every billionaire in the United States to make up for the unjust tax burden placed upon their shoulders for untold years. We think that a formula that would give to each and every needy billionaire a one-time payment of one and one-half times his current net worth would, for the time being, be adequate. For example, a person who has a current net worth of five billion dollars would be awarded a check of $7.5 billion. Although we realize that this does not come close to the losses incurred by America's billionaires, it is, we believe, a good starting point. The total amount for the reparations to all of the billionaires would only come to approximately $2,250,000,000,000 ($2.25 trillion). This sum of money could easily be obtained by dipping into Social Security and Medicare, and by increasing the tax rate on the useless poor and the slow-witted middle class.

In conclusion, we demand that the punitive and criminal tax scheme levied against the vulnerable super-rich end immediately! The billionaires of the United States are being punished for being superior; the poor are being rewarded for being lazy and stupid. It is time for this ruthless government tyranny against the oppressed billionaire to be abolished forever!

SOCIALISM FOR THE RICH

CAPITALISM FOR THE POOR

YOU GOT A PROBLEM WITH THAT?

Once I owned half of New York City, but now it's done.
Brother, can you spare a measly $72 million?

-Baleful refrain heard on Wall Street

the day of the great stock market

crash of 1929

Once I owned half of New York City, but now it's done.
American taxpayers, can you spare several hundred billion
dollars?

-Baleful refrain heard on Wall Street the

day the super-rich became firm believers

in socialism – for themselves, that is.

THE GREED SCORECARD

NET WORTH

FORBES 400 GANG: $1,500,000,000,000

SATAN: $666,666,666,666

BILL GATES: $59,000,000,000

WARREN BUFFETT: $39,000,000,000

JIM C. WALTON: $21,100,000,000

MICHAEL BLOOMBERG: $19,500,000,000

RUPERT MURDOCH: $7,400,000,000

OPRAH WINFREY: $2,700,000,000

JESUS: $0

HONORABLE MENTION

GANDHI

(net worth)

A pair or worn-out sandals and an

assassin's bullet to the gut.

THE APOSTLE MATTHEW

(net worth)

A leaky water flask and an

old, gimpy donkey.

MOTHER THERESA

(net worth)

Is a used nun's habit worth anything?

THE THREE PENNY OPERA

THE WALMART BLUES

Sixteen years and what do you get?

Another year older and deeper in debt

Let me tell you mister how I got so poor

I owe my soul to the Walmart store.

I've got a bad heart, bad teeth,

and two flat feet

But without health insurance there ain't

one I can treat

So I hobble around Walmart trying

to do my chores

While the Walton family fortune

continues to soar.

If you see Walmart coming better step aside

A lot of workers didn't and a lot of them cried

One day working there and you'll get your fill

If the low wages don't get ya the meager benefits will.

Sixteen years and what do you get?

Another year older and deeper in debt

Let me tell you mister how I got so poor

I owe my soul to the Walmart store.

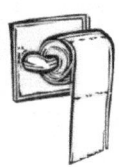

THE GREED STREET JOURNAL

AN INTERVIEW WITH DR. MALTON FRAUDMAN

CHAIR OF THE ECONOMICS DEPARTMENT

IN THE FREEDOM GRADUATE SCHOOL

OF FREEMARKET ECONOMICS

AT PATRIOT UNIVERSITY

INTERVIEWED BY STEVE FARBES

Steve Farbes:

Thank you Dr. Fraudman for granting us this interview.
We know what a hectic schedule you have.

Dr. Fraudman:

You are more than welcome, Steve. I have weighed the
opportunity cost of devoting an hour to this interview as
opposed to attending the invitation-only $10,000-per-plate
dinner at Patriot University's yearly "Free Market Freedom
Festival" and have determined that I will profit more by
speaking to you than by attending the festival by
approximately $123.65.

Steve Farbes:

You are an extremely rational and analytical person, Dr. Fraudman. I have to say, at the risk of shameless fawning, that I am in awe of your greatness.

Dr. Fraudman:

This is very nice of you to say, Steve. It is true, I am great, but I do have to say that I would give away my unparalleled intellect, all of my money and even my wife and children if I could only be five inches taller. You see, I am only 5'2".

Steve Farbes:

I didn't notice that you are vertically challenged.

Dr. Fraudman:

You do realize that I am not sitting, but standing?

Steve Farbes:

Oh. Well, anyway, the reason we are here today is to learn your opinion on the subject of corporate taxation. As you are well aware, there has been an effort of late by the lily-livered, pinko-commie, America-hating liberals to raise the tax rate ceiling on the lifeblood of our great God-fearing nation, the mega-rich corporation. Level-headed politicians on the right have attempted to stave off this push, but they are embattled by the stupid and angry American masses. What are your thoughts on this issue?

Dr. Fraudman:

First off, let me say that I have no political affiliations whatsoever. I have no axe to grind. My only motive is to arrive at a solution that will be the most advantageous for each and every millionaire and billionaire in our great freedom-loving country.

Steve Farbes:

This is quite admirable, Dr. Fraudman. So many evil-minded socialists on the left seem to be solely motivated by the idea of lining the empty pockets of the greedy poor and destitute but never give the slightest consideration to the plight of American's astronomically wealthy mega corporations.

Dr. Fraudman:

Come now Steve, let's not cast aspersions at the left for merely having a difference of opinion on the complex issue of corporate taxation. Those on the left are in no way evil or malicious. They truly want to bring about a solution that will bring about a prosperity that will spread across all strata of America's diverse population. I say again, they are not evil; they are simply extraordinarily dumb. They simply do not have the intellectual capacity to understand an economic problem of this complexity. Attempting to explain the reality of the effects of burdensome taxes on a corporation to a slow-witted liberal is like trying to explain Einstein's *Theory of Relativity* to a retarded turtle. There is simply no way that you can get through to them; consequently, one should not become angry at them because of their ignorance and lack of understanding. One should simply let them rant and rave like spoiled little children while one smiles and reassuringly pats them atop their vacuous heads as one simultaneously inserts a lollypop into their rapacious little mouths to end the senseless chatter.

Steve Farbes:

This is a most noble and enlightened approach to dealing with the annoyingly persistent blathering of the feeble-minded bleeding hearts.

Dr. Fraudman:

Yes, it is. Now, in regards to your question pertaining to a hike in taxes on corporations, I can say without any equivocation that I am wholeheartedly opposed to the proposition. It goes without saying that an increase in taxes on corporations would be disastrous to both the corporations and the economy as a whole.

Steve Farbes:

Would you then propose a reduction, rather than an increase, in the corporate tax rate?

Dr. Fraudman:

Absolutely.

Steve Farbes:

To what level: 25%, 20%, 18%?

Dr. Fraudman:

Zero.

Steve Farbes:

Excuse me, did you say zero?

Dr. Fraudman:

Yes, I did.

Steve Farbes:

That is a very interesting idea, Dr. Fraudman. Please explain your rationale.

Dr. Fraudman:

Certainly. It is obvious that the driving force of our economy is the mega corporation. As the mega corporation goes, so goes the U.S. economy. Now, what would happen if the tax rate were cut to zero as opposed to increasing it to the Soviet-style level proposed by the left? With a tax rate of zero, all of the money that would have been put into such impractical, pie-in-the-sky projects such as building roads, repairing crumbling bridges, and providing meals to starving children, could instead be reintroduced into the corporations. This influx of funds would necessarily fuel expansion of the corporations and by extension, through a trickle-down effect akin to delicious crumbs falling off of a king's table down to the starving masses below, the expansion and growth of the U.S. economy in general.

Steve Farbes:

The elimination of corporate taxes would lead to a dramatic decrease in tax revenues and thereby a reduction in social programs for the poor. How would you respond to those bleeding hearts who say that without a handout from the government, countless children would starve?

Dr. Fraudman:

Poppycock. Nothing could be further from the truth. Let's examine this logically. If corporate taxes were eliminated, corporate profits would necessarily increase which would result in a dramatic rise in the net worth of the executives who run the companies. Being so flush with almost unlimited wealth, these executives would feel the need to give back to all of the little, insignificant people. As such, they would, as Rockefeller did in the old days, fill their cashmere pockets full of shiny nickels and dimes which they would generously shower down on the ground to the desperate little starving children. With this precious money, these filthy children could purchase food staples and even tooth-rotting soda pop and lemon drops.

Steve Farbes:

This is supremely logical, Dr. Fraudman, but how do we convince the irrational and unpredictable masses that your plan is the best solution for all?

Dr. Fraudman:

We don't. We simply implement the changes despite their protests.

Steve Farbes:

But this could lead to riots.

Dr. Fraudman:

Very likely, but any sort of rebellion could be easily crushed by the U.S. military, or better yet, private mercenary forces paid for by American tax dollars. You would be surprised how persuasive an armored vehicle and an assault rifle can be.

Steve Farbes:

Sometimes tough love is the best kind of love.

Dr. Fraudman:

Exactly. If the masses are too obtuse to be reasoned with then they must be "corrected" at the end of a gun barrel.

Steve Farbes:

Well, thank you Dr. Fraudman. As usual, your observations are both insightful and impeccably logical.

Dr. Fraudman:

Thank you, Steve. Now, if you will please excuse me, I have to go home and perform some complicated calculations to determine if feeding starving orphans in Romania is Pareto efficient or if it would make more economic sense to simply allow them to die.

THE DEVIL'S DICTIONARY

BLEEDING HEART: A phrase that is commonly used by those members of the political spectrum on the extreme right. It describes a person who senselessly cares about his fellow human beings. It is applied to a person who, for whatever peculiar reason, has compassion for those who are less fortunate than himself. It describes an individual who thinks not of his own welfare and self-interest but instead needlessly sacrifices his time, energy, and even part of his wealth to those in desperate need.

Synonyms

Compassion; sympathy; empathy

Antonyms

Asshole; prick; dick

Historical figures who were bleeding hearts

Jesus; Gandhi; Mother Theresa

Historical figures who were not

Hitler; Genghis Khan; Caligula

Usage

-The moronic *bleeding heart* liberal gave five dollars to the desperate homeless man.

-The Brazilian authorities imprisoned the *bleeding heart* fool who protested the destruction of millions of acres of irreplaceable rain forest.

-The uninsured cancer patient was able to receive medical treatment through a foolish donation from some lame-brained *bleeding heart*.

LET GREEDOM RING!

Let greedom ring from the posh luxury apartments of New York City!

Let greedom ring from the roads paved in gold in Beverly Hills!

But not only that; let greedom ring from the ghetto wastelands of Detroit!

Let greedom ring from the winding unemployment lines of Cleveland!

Let greedom ring from every sweatshop and every prison in Bangladesh.

From every country, let greedom ring.

When we let greedom ring,

When we let it ring from every village and every hamlet,

From every state and every city,

We will be able to speed up that day when we will enslave ALL of God's children,

Black men and white men,

Jews and Gentiles,

Protestants and Catholics,

While we plutocrats join hands and sing the old capitalist anthem,

"Greed at last!

 Greed at last!

 Thank Satan almighty we have greed at last!"

Let the middle class and poor tremble at the capitalist revolution. Insatiable billionaires of the world unite! You have nothing to lose but your souls; you have a world of desperate working-class poor to enslave.

-The Capitalist Manifesto

THE GREED STREET JOURNAL

OP-ED

BY

Dr. Judas Benedict Sophistrous

Senior Obfuscator

At the Herbert Huver Institute of Dubious Studies

"WALMART: THE SMALL BUSINESS OWNER'S
BEST FRIEND"

MAY 14, 1992

A great deal of controversy has recently surrounded the
arrival of the non-union super store, Walmart, into
communities across the United States. The greatest concern
has arisen from small business owners who feel that they
will be in direct competition with the superstore. The
apparent fear is that being a small business, they will not be
able to compete successfully with a large, national chain;
however, it can said without equivocation that nothing
could be further from the truth. The arrival of a Walmart
store in an area will help small businesses, not hurt them. I
am supported in this position by the renowned scholar

Walter Fink of the non-partisan think tank "*Death to All Small Businesses*" who says that "the introduction of an un-unionized Walmart in an area will provide the economic stimulus that will lead to an influx of capital, investment and consumers, thereby increasing, not decreasing, business activity of the small business owner." Mr. Fink points out that Walmart will complement its small business competition, not compete with it. "The people who frequent a large discount store such as Walmart do not represent the same demographic as those who frequent a mom and pop store. Business owners and consumers alike should welcome with open arms the arrival of a Walmart into their community" adds Mr. Fink.

There has also been concern expressed by workers that having a massive, multinational superstore in their town that does not allow its employees to unionize will have an adverse effect on the power of unions and thereby negatively affect both wages and benefits. Mr. Fink, supported by in depth research at the *Institute for the Destruction of Labor Unions*, responds, "Those who think upon those lines do not have an understanding of fundamental economic principles. People always have a choice in the type of work in which they employ themselves. This is the beauty of our extremist, capitalist system." Mr. Fink goes on to say, " If a prospective worker disapproves of non-union businesses, he has the choice to either go contrary to his principles and work at a non-union company such as Walmart, or he may bypass the opportunity and instead stay home on his barcalounger and watch *The Price is Right* and reruns of *The Joker's Wild*. In either case, it's his choice: earning a very generous subsistence living at Walmart, or enduring the misery, disease and untimely death that abject poverty and perpetual unemployment so generously provide.

So, put your feeble minds at ease dear workers and small business owners. Like an unstoppable Nazi blitzkrieg into Poland, benevolent Walmart is coming to a location near you.

LIFESTYLES OF THE POOR AND NAMELESS

Welcome to *Lifestyles of the Poor and Nameless*.

My name is Robber Baron Leach.

On today's show, we head down to rural Arkansas to the "residence" of Joe and Mable Thorpe. Joe and Mable recently lost their home through foreclosure, so they are now residing in the back of their rusted-out econoline cargo van with their three cats, Whimsy, Mr. Boots, and Sir Chesterfield the Third. This may sound like a tragic turn of events, but it is all cool because now they are a closer family than they have ever been before. Of course, having only fifty square feet in which to live for Mom, Dad, their son Bucky and their three cats does present some minor problems; for example, the necessity of placing the cats' litter box next to young Bucky's pillow can sometimes be a challenge, especially when Mr. Boots decides to take a massive crap at three in the morning, or when Sir Chesterfield's aim is a tad off and he misses the box all together. But hey, don't worry, be happy! As they say, no matter how bad life gets, there is always someone in the world enduring more dire circumstances than you. Well, maybe not in the case of the Thorpes, but you get the idea.

In any event, ever since Mr. Thorpe's job at the mill was exported to New Delhi, India, he has been unable to find employment. Recently, he failed to land the highly prized job of cart guy at the local Piggly Wiggly supermarket. Surprisingly enough, he lost out to some sixteen-year-old high school dropout. Mr. Thorpe thinks that perhaps he was unable to secure this position because on his job application, in the address section, he wrote, "crappy old van parked next to the dumpster behind the Super Kmart". He won't make that mistake again.

Everything is not all doom and gloom, however; for example, last week, Mr. Thorpe's eight-year-old son, Bucky, climbed into the Kmart dumpster at his father's behest in pursuit of a tasty morsel of food. After wading through a seemingly interminable mountain of paper, dirt, and Grey Poupon mustard, young Bucky, by this time yellow from head to toe, emerged with a package of Keebler cookies and a gallon of spoiled skim milk. The Thorpe's enjoyed a far, far better repast that evening than they had had in weeks.

Unfortunately, during Bucky's descent into dumpster hell, he stepped on a rusty nail, and his foot became horribly infected. Having lost their medical insurance coverage, Mrs. Thorpe found it necessary to resort to traditional medical techniques to heal her son. That evening, she dug up what she thought was the root of the goldenseal plant, made a strong tea from it, and had her ailing son drink several cups of the steaming brew. Inexplicably, Bucky soon after became deathly ill. Not being a trained herbalist, Mrs. Thorpe immediately realized that there was the distinct possibility that she had had her beloved son drink not the tea of the medicinal goldenseal, but instead deadly hemlock. When their son's legs became paralyzed and heavier than a bucket of lead, she knew she had made an awful mistake. As the numbness steadily traveled up towards Bucky's heart, they rushed him to the nearby clinic; unfortunately, they were too late, and he died later that night.

Despite this tragic turn of events, the Thorpe's of late seem to be getting their lives back on track; Mr. Thorpe, for example, is checking out the possibility of donating his plasma and semen three times a week at $30 a pop, and dear Mrs. Thorpe is seriously thinking of becoming a street whore. Yes, things are really looking up for the Thorpes.

Well, ladies and gentlemen, that's our show for this week. Next week, we'll travel to Detroit, Michigan, to the home of a black woman who has been without heat in her apartment since the coldest winter in history gripped the city two and a half months ago.

And until we meet again, I wish you "Flat beer wishes and generic peanut butter dreams"!

A DAY IN THE LIFE

OF

OPRAH WINFREY & A TOMATO PICKER

5:00 A.M.

OPRAH

Sleeps

TOMATO PICKER

She awakens sandwiched between her grabby-hands uncle Pepe and her gassy grandpa Juan.

7:00 A.M.

OPRAH

Sleeps.

TOMATO PICKER

Arrives at work in the back of some hillbilly's pickup truck with ten other drones.

9:00 A.M.

OPRAH

Awakens beneath luxurious silk sheets. Contemplates how wonderful she is as she dreamily stares up at the coiffured, gold-leaf ceiling above.

TOMATO PICKER

Contemplates suicide for the third time since starting work. Thinks that leaving Cuernavaca, Mexico may have been a humungous mistake.

11.00 A.M.

OPRAH

Arrives at office in limousine. Complains that the Perrier water is 1.75 degrees warmer than it should be.

TOMATO PICKER

Extreme thirst and exhaustion grip her. Fantasizes about someone repeatedly striking her atop the head with a shovel to end her unceasing misery.

NOON

OPRAH

Two-hour "working" lunch commences.

TOMATO PICKER

A pot of hot slop is carted out to the workers. Our protagonist greedily consumes the steaming gruel.

2:00 P.M.

OPRAH

"Working" lunch ends. Time for a nap.

TOMATO PICKER

Sexually harassed by perverted foreman.

4:00 P.M.

OPRAH

Wakes for filming of show. Reads through pre-written questions.

TOMATO PICKER

Ten-minute water break. Too tired to converse with fellow slaves.

5:00 P.M.

OPRAH

Filming of show. Crowd can barely contain their excitement over her greatness.

TOMATO PICKER

End of work day. Driven back to town and pushed off truck.

6:00 P.M.

OPRAH

Receives $750,000 check for a hard day's work. Seriously considers asking for a pay raise.

TOMATO PICKER

Crashes on Salvation Army futon. Falls asleep immediately.

7:00 P.M.

OPRAH

Returns home by private helicopter. Balls out gardener for planting too many roses and not enough lilac bushes.

TOMATO PICKER

Awakens. Reflexively turns on recorded Oprah show.

THE ENCANTING TALE OF

"THE UNENDING LABORS OF SISYPHUS"

Once upon a time there lived a man by the name of Sisyphus. Since the time poor Sisyphus was eighteen years of age, he had dutifully performed his job at the rock quarry. Receiving a paltry sum of money for the difficult, dirty and dangerous job he was required to perform, the now aged and used up Sisyphus nevertheless smiled through it all, comforted by the knowledge that one day his ceaseless life of drudgery would end and he would be rewarded with a life of frugal leisure.

One day his blessed retirement arrived and Sisyphus's heart was filled with an overwhelming feeling of relief and unbounded joy. After 47 years of slavery, he was finally to receive his just rewards. Although Sisyphus had dutifully worked forty-seven long years, he was still surprisingly a man of very limited means. Sending his two children off to the state college with its skyrocketing tuition nearly wiped out his cash reserves, and his battle with a medical condition that was not fully covered by his multinational corporation's watered-down health insurance plan nearly brought him to the precipice of financial ruin; however, he had somehow weathered both of these storms and now found himself at the end of his career in a tenuous financial position. Sisyphus's heart nevertheless was light, for he knew that if he lived the life of a Hindu ascetic, abstaining from all frivolous luxuries such as Hellmann's mayonnaise and Coco Puffs cereal, that he could live out the rest of his uneventful life in peace and comfortable monotony.

Soon after leaving his job and settling into his new life of inexpensive activities and entertainments - such as watching three-hour stretches of Judge Judy, Judge Mathis, and Judge Joe Brown, and reading the free daily newspaper in the local library - Sisyphus became aware that his social security check had not yet arrived in the mail. Not knowing what to do, Sisyphus called the Social Security Administration office to discover the reason. The woman to whom he spoke informed him in a mechanical tone of voice that no more social security checks would be sent out ever again. Sisyphus swallowed hard as beads of sweat appeared on his wrinkled and worried brow.

"But how could this be?" pleaded the now desperate Sisyphus.

The woman, bored beyond comprehension for having repeated this same scripted message to one hundred thousand other devastated retirees, continued,

"The Supreme Court of the United States has determined that both Social Security and Medicare are unconstitutional and have therefore abolished both programs."

Sisyphus was unaware that a consortium of billionaire plutocrats had bribed a powerful and influential congressmen to file suit for the abolition of all "entitlements" to the greedy poor. The passage of the new law received enthusiastic support from all of the millionaires, billionaires, wealthy lawmakers and many of the brainwashed masses who had their TV sets permanently tuned in to Fox News.

Sisyphus, not knowing what to do, spent the remainder of the day contemplating shooting himself in the head with the newly legalized UZI or drowning himself in the kitchen sink. Realizing that he didn't have enough money to buy an UZI and being unable to locate the sink stopper, Sisyphus decided that he had to return to work. He attempted to regain his former job at the rock quarry, but was told that there were no openings; however, Sisyphus was no fool. He realized that the reason he was not rehired was that at his age, the cost of his health insurance would be too high for the mind-bogglingly rich corporation.

After two months of desperately searching for any kind of employment, Sisyphus was lucky enough to secure the position of manservant, a.k.a. "house bitch", at the luxurious mansion of Congressman Hoover, the selfsame person who had spearheaded the legislation that abolished Social Security and Medicare. Although the cantankerous and demanding congressman refused to provide the aging Sisyphus with medical insurance, he did pay him the competitive wage of $3.25 per hour. (Congressman Hoover was also the driving force behind the abolition of the minimum wage). Although Sisyphus had envisioned himself enjoying his later years receiving senior-discounted coffees at McDonald's intermixed with the occasional big mouth bass fishing expedition to the local reservoir, he instead found himself helping Congressman Hoover change his underpants three times per day.

When asked if there was any bitterness or resentment towards the Congressman for his part in the abolition of a safety net into which he had faithfully paid for forty-seven years, the normally quiet and respectful Sisyphus responded,

"What the fuc* do you think?"

It would seem that there was a note of displeasure in his response, but perhaps if he had been aware that the hundreds of billions of dollars that have been saved by not paying senior citizens what they rightly earned and deserve has provided the United States with sufficient funds to invade, destroy, and occupy two oil-laden Middle Eastern countries, it would perhaps put his mind at ease. So, as we can plainly see, everything has worked out for the best.

THE DEVIL'S DICTIONARY

BLOOD IN THE STREETS: a phrase used by the parasitic, blood-sucking billionaire opportunists to describe a situation in which excessive profits can be made during a severe economic crisis. It is most advantageous if chaos ensues, that is desperation, hopelessness, starvation and death among the irrational masses. This allows the cool-headed billionaire to snatch up bargains. It describes a situation in which the vast majority of the country is suffering and/or dying while the billionaire achieves greater and greater economic gains.

Usage

Knowing that the businessman was in an extremely desperate financial situation, the billionaire offered to buy the assets of his business for 10% of their actual worth.

Synonyms

Capitalism; free-market economics.

A DAY IN THE LIFE

OF

DONALD TRUMP

&

A HOUSEKEEPER AT TRUMP TOWER

6:00 A.M.

TRUMP

Sleeps completely naked on the other side of mountainous pillow barrier between him and his fully-clothed trophy wife.

HOUSEKEEPER

Arrives at work and is immediately commanded to clean up gigantic puke accident on the twelfth floor.

8:00 A.M.

TRUMP

Enters massive walk-in closet. Can't decide which of his five hundred $3,000 Italian suites to wear.

HOUSEKEEPER

Scrubs dirty toilet bowl for the 99,000th time.

9:30 A.M.

TRUMP

While staring into mirror, practices saying "You're fired!" over and over again.

HOUSEKEEPER

Enters room 237. Catches ugly couple having sex on the floor. Male asks if she would care to join them.

10:00 A.M.

TRUMP

Scrutinizes the cleanliness of the hotel lobby. Not totally satisfied with the shine on the marble columns.

HOUSEKEEPER

Has usual morning gasping attack after inhaling poisonous, vaporized tub & tile cleaner.

11.30 A.M.

TRUMP

Has meeting with high-powered lawyers to determine if there is any way he could legally have Rosie O'Donald murdered.

HOUSEKEEPER

Due to overpowering hunger, samples a half-eaten croissant left behind by some bored billionaire. Detects unusual almond aftertaste. Dizziness and heart palpitations commence.

NOON

TRUMP

Becoming testy because he has yet to fire anyone this morning.

HOUSEKEEPER

Violently ill. Passes out while leaning over to pick up a used condom. Housekeeping supervisor catches her slacking off. Vows to inform Trump.

12:01 P.M.

TRUMP

Fires Housekeeper

AT THE MOVIES WITH STEVE FARBES

REVIEW OF

A CHRISTMAS CAROL

BY

CHARLES DICKENS

Set in the ebullient and exciting time of the Industrial Revolution in merry old Victorian London, the story begins in the reputable and orderly business establishment of one Mr. Ebenezer Scrooge. From the opening scene onward, the movie is positively popping with witty repartee and profoundly wise observations of the part of the level-headed and business-like Mr. Scrooge. In one of its many lively exchanges, his lazy and ungrateful employee, Bob Cratchit, attempts to clandestinely place a piece of expensive coal into the fireplace. Fortunately, the ever-watchful Mr. Scrooge spies him doing so and reprimands the thief, informing him that the cold is what jackets are for.

Soon after setting Cratchit straight, two uninvited socialist parasites enter his place of business and attempt to extort money from the frugal Mr. Scrooge. Unmoved by the two leaches' sentimental entreaties concerning feeding the poor

325

at Christmas, Ebenezer forthrightly tells the two bums that he shall not even donate a single farthing towards their ill-advised cause as there are a sufficient number of prisons and workhouses where the unfortunate members of society can find relief.

After a hard day's work, Scrooge finds himself back home later that evening. While eating a bowl of wholesome gruel, the ghost of what appears to be his dead business partner, Jacob Marley, unexpectedly visits him. At first, Scrooge is unsure that what he sees is real, thinking that the apparition before him may simply be a piece of undercooked beef (prepared by an illegal immigrant or perhaps a Jew). After a seemingly interminable stretch of time in which the merciless ghost rants and raves insanely about "mankind" being his business, Scrooge is coerced, by cruel scare tactics, to admit that the ghost does indeed exist. While watching this disturbing scene, one is, however, heartened when one sees that the ghost carries around with him many heavy money boxes, proving without a doubt that even after death we can take our riches with us.

Soon after the disappearance of the annoying apparition, Scrooge wisely bellows "Bah humbug" and retires to his comfy bed; however, a peaceful night of slumber is not to be for the personable Mr. Scrooge. At the stroke of midnight, Ebenezer is rudely awoken by the Ghost of Christmas Past. Without even allowing Scrooge to put on an overcoat, this foolish spirit transports him through space and time, showing him various scenes from his past. At one point, he is magically whisked through the air to a frivolous party that is taking place on the premises of his moronic former employer, Fezziwig. Scrooge is thereafter flown through the air and compelled to relive a tongue-lashing from his demanding and sentimental bride-to-be. Wisely, Scrooge from the past pays no heed to her wishy-washy rant on love and fixes his sites on a fulfilling life of cold, calculating, and selfish commerce. As one watches these scenes, one realizes that the obvious moral that Dickens is attempting to convey is that love, charity, and generosity are foolish sentiments that should never interfere with the relentless pursuit of wealth.

After the departure of the apparition, Scrooge utters a series of "bah humbugs!" and retires to his bed. Soon after closing his eyes, he is once again rudely awoken, this time by the Ghost of Christmas Present. This overweight and uncouth spirit, gaudily clad in a discordant array of raiments, kidnaps Scrooge, taking him against his will to the home of his lazy employee, Bob Cratchit. In this dark and dank hovel, Scrooge has to endure the vitriol of Cratchit's bitchy and ungrateful wife and the disturbing appearance of a gimp by the name of Tiny Tim. Young Tim, as handicapped mentally as he is physically, hobbles about the residence in an exaggerated manner (a routine which has obviously been taught to him by his father in order to elicit unwarranted sympathy and handouts form the hard-working businessmen of London.) The Ghost of Christmas Present informs Ebenezer that if things remain unchanged, he sees an empty chair where Tiny Tim rests his scrawny legs. This of course may be unfortunate in a bleeding-heart liberal sort of way, but from a practical, business-like standpoint, it is desirable for the worthless Tim to die because, due to his physical inferiority, he would be a financial burden on society his entire life. Unfortunately, upon hearing of the approaching demise of the lame Tim, Scrooge unwisely begins to waver in his longstanding and steadfast conviction that Tiny Tim and his kind should not be given one tax-payer pence or gift of charity due to their condition, but instead should earn their keep by working in a coal mine or by descending down a soot-filled chimney until merciful death wrests them from this earthly plane.

After once again retiring to bed, Scrooge is visited by a final spirit, the Ghost of Christmas Yet to Come. By this point in the story, the inhumane scare tactics of the two previous spirits compel him to descend into a socialist hell. The shrouded, Grim Reaper-like Ghost of Christmas Yet to Come – an obvious allusion to the looming specter of communism – in typical totalitarian fashion, threatens Mr. Scrooge with his own untimely demise in order to coerce him into adopting a warped liberal ideology.

Upon waking from his "dream", Ebenezer Scrooge thoroughly embarrasses himself by giddily greeting everyone he meets with a hardy, heartfelt "Merry Christmas", overpaying for a freakishly large turkey for the useless Cratchit family, and becoming a benefactor to the lame and worthless Tiny Tim, who, through unearned and undeserved financial assistance, survives.

RATING: $

Rating key

$$$$: Excellent

$$$: Good

$$: Fair

$: Obvious vehicle for socialist ideology

The balcony is closed to anyone with a net worth less than $100 million.

SPREADING THE WEALTH

THE FORBES 300 MILLION

All of the statistics have been calculated and compiled and

CONGRATULATIONS!!!

The chances are very good that you have made the list of one of the 300 million richest people in the United States!

Mr. and Mrs. Average American, you've just discovered that you're as rich as 300 million other people in this country. What are you going to do now?

Answer: Absolutely nothing!!

Unfortunately, in a country of 310 million people, some of you didn't quite make it onto this august list of financial titans. Here are just a couple of examples of the 10 million people who did not quite have the financial clout to make the list:

Marge and Stanley Foreclosure

Who lost their house and now find themselves living in their lovely classic car.

Samuel Outcast

Former high school track star, who now takes up residence on the sidewalk at the corner of Superior and 5th.

THE ENCHANTING TALE OF

"THE HEDGE FUND MANAGER AND THE BUM"

Once upon a time in the fair metropolis of Gotham, there lived a greedy ogre by the name of Jon Palson. One cold and blustery day in November, Ogre Palson, on his way to "work", exited from the back of his luxurious limousine and noticed the approach of a foul-looking, no-good street bum. This Ogre, ever on guard against his arch enemies, the poor and downtrodden, quickly reached into his cashmere overcoat pocket and grasped his trusty bottle of hot pepper spray. The homeless man, clad in an old and tattered Kmart blue-light special jacket, mud-stained trousers, and shoes not fit for a church rummage sale, plodded towards Ogre Palson with upturned palm.

"Please sir, can you spare a dollar?" pleaded the pathetic man.

Ogre Palson, studying the dirty man before him, became enraged that this wretch would have the audacity to demand money from him.

Why would this disgusting leach not simply drop dead on the spot and do everyone in fair Gotham a favor thought Ogre Palson.

"Please sir," continued the bum, "if you could find it in your heart to help a poor soul who has fallen on hard times. You see, I have not always lived a life such as this. Once, I was much like you."

Ogre Palson, unimpressed with the bum's pathos, clutched the pepper spray even tighter in his angry right hand.

"You see, I was one of the many victims of the collapse of the home mortgage market," the bum continued. "One day I had a home, a family, and a life; the next, I lost my home, my marriage, and any reason to live."

It was at this juncture that the bum, overwhelmed with emotion, began to sob uncontrollably. Ogre Palson, seizing the opportunity, whipped out the pepper spray from his pocket, pointed it directly at the homeless man's tear-filled eyes, and blinded him with the fiery liquid. Shrieks of agonized pain issued from the bum as he desperately rubbed his inflamed eyes in vain. Feeling pleased that he had subdued the pushy street rat, Ogre Palson watched with great satisfaction as the pathetic man writhed in pain. Spying a passing beat cop, Ogre Palson waved him over.

"Arrest this vicious animal, officer. He threatened me with bodily violence," demanded the self-righteous Ogre.

The cop, seeing how expensively Ogre Palson was dressed, quickly deduced that he must be telling the truth. In the blink of an eye, the bum found himself face down in the frigid snow with handcuffs around his wrists.

"Off to jail for him, I should think," chuckled Ogre Palson to the arresting officer.

"Or a mental institution for 'observation,'" responded the officer.

Ogre Palson smiled as he said, "Yes, a for-profit penitentiary or a for-profit psychiatric facility is what he requires. Whichever is more profitable to the respective institution."

The officer nodded in agreement before throwing the battered bum into the back of a police cruiser. As the vehicle sped away, Ogre Palson's ever-loyal chauffeur approached him.

"Are you alright, sir?" inquired the subservient, minimum-wage employee.

"Yes, my faithful slave. I am fine," responded Ogre Palson as he adjusted the 24-carat gold tie clip that, if sold at any pawn shop in town, would provide sufficient funds to feed and shelter the now jail-bound bum for several months. It was at this point in time that the chauffeur became suddenly pensive. After a few moments of painful cogitation, the chauffeur said,

"Sir, do you think it's possible that that man could have been one of the victims of the collapsing home mortgage market that you sold short on?"

With a sly smile appearing on his face, Ogre Palson playfully winked at the chauffeur. Turning up his collar to the cold November wind, Ogre Palson contentedly made his way into the towering office building, all the while dreaming of new and more diabolical ways to screw his fellow human beings.

The moral of the story: WHITE COLLAR CRIME PAYS

October 8, 1888

Classified Advertisement

Wanted:

Labourers for employment at the Lucifer Match Manufacturer, Shoreditch, London. Fourteen-hour shifts with one allotted ten-minute break. Compensation is 3 shillings 9 pence per week. Work week is Monday through Saturday with a generous half day off on Sunday. Work commences promptly at 4 A.M., rain or shine. Those interested in this fine opportunity should arrive outside the manufacturer this coming Saturday at which time the foreman, a Mr. Daniel Quilp, will make his selections from amongst the desperate masses. The ideal candidate is either a strapping homeless lad or lass of tender age - 7-10 is ideal - or a desperate woman with no other employment opportunities other than perhaps that of a street whore. Temperatures within the building can approach 110 degrees, so dress accordingly. (Ladies are required to keep their entire bodies completely covered at all times for decency's sake.)

Any attempt at pinching a bob from our till will result in the whip man administering a *violent scroby* upon the criminal's back until plenteous blood does issue forth.

Sickness, infirmity, or impending death or any other hookem-snivey that prevents the worker from putting in a full day's labour *will not be tolerated* and will be grounds for IMMEDIATE TERMINATION from employment.

A wholesome skilly of wild purslane and eel-head soup will be provided at 2 pence per ladle. A slice of wheat-chaff bread will be 1 pence extra.

Any attempt to organize the labourers into a worker's union will be dealt with in the

severest possible manner.

THE THREE PENNY OPERA

THOSE WERE THE DAYS

The 1800's were the days

Free enterprise held total sway

Crooks like us, we had it made

Those were the days.

Didn't need no welfare state

The mindless masses pulled all the weight

Gee, child labor sure was great

Those were the days.

You could pay just pennies then

To desperate women, boys, girls and men

And those who griped were sent to the pen

Those were the days.

And you knew your millions then

Wouldn't go to kids begging for bread

Mister, we could use some more dead union leaders again.

Didn't need no safety net

Being unemployed meant certain death

But hey, we plutocrats were set

Those were the days!

CONGRATULATIONS!

THE GREED HALL OF FAME'S ANNUAL
AWARDS CEREMONY

BEING HELD ON THE LUXURIOUS
GROUNDS OF THE MEPHISTOPHELES
HOTEL IN NEW YORK CITY

PROUDLY PRESENTS THIS YEAR'S
INDUCTEE

JOHN PAULSON

2007 "EARNINGS": $3.5 BILLION

2008 "EARNINGS": $3 BILLION

2010 "EARNINGS": $4.9 BILLION

TOTAL NET WORTH: $15.5 BILLION

(MADE DURING THE WORST FINANCIAL
CRISIS SINCE THE GREAT DEPRESSION.)

This year's inductee is distinguished by his unparalleled selfishness in the face of widespread hardship and suffering. Difficult is it for this august body of rapaciously greedy capitalists to recall an individual who has so brazenly hoarded his ill-begotten wealth in the midst of a sea of financial disaster. Such selfish courage is and shall be for generations of avaricious capitalists to come an enduring inspiration and example of the extent to which one can live the life of a king while surrounded by the countless destitute and poor.

BRAVO, MR. PAULSON!

WHO WANTS TO BE A BILLIONAIRE?

INT. STUDIO / NIGHT

ENTER: REGIS HASBIN & JOHN PAULSON

Regis Hasbin

Welcome to *Who Wants To Be A Billionaire*? On today's show, we have Wall Street hedge fund manager extraordinaire, John Paulson. Welcome to the show Mr. Paulson.

John Paulson

Thank you.

Regis Hasbin

May I call you John?

John Paulson

No.

Regis Hasbin

Oh. Anyway, for those of you in our viewing audience who are not familiar with Mr. Paulson, a short bio is in order. He is that blood sucker who made billions of dollars selling short on the subprime home mortgage market. In effect, he placed his bet on the hope that the home mortgage market would collapse. Is this correct, Mr. Paulson?

John Paulson

Essentially

Regis Hasbin

Sucking the life blood out of your country and into your personal bank account must have been quite a rush.

John Paulson

It was better than murder, I mean sex. Although I must say that I spent many a sleepless night worrying, hoping and praying that the home mortgage market would collapse, and fortunately, one day it did.

The stage manager holds up an applause sign. Riotous applause erupts from the brain-dead audience.

Regis Hasbin

Profiting off of other people's misery, that is the capitalist's fondest dream; however, do you ever have any moments in which you regret that you made billions of dollars off of a collapsing market that lead to thousands of people losing their homes?

The stage manager holds up a "boo" sign. The obedient audience immediately responds with cacophonous boos, sneers, and hisses. Paulson shakes his head in disbelief at the inane question.

John Paulson

Absolutely not. My profits were simply the result of the free market functioning as it should. As you know, I am a firm believer in the free market: I'm free to make billions and others are free to become suddenly homeless. You see how beautifully the system works?

An applause sign is held up. The obsequious audience applauds.

Regis Hasbin

Yes, it is all perfectly clear now. Anyway, are you ready to play our game for a chance to win one billion dollars?

John Paulson

Absolutely.

Regis Hasbin

Then, let's play *Who Wants to be a Billionaire?* Your first question is for one million dollars:

How many parasitic billionaires does it take to loot a country of $1.5 trillion?

  A) One million
  B) One hundred thousand
  C) Ten thousand
  D) Four hundred

John Paulson

D, four hundred.

Regis Hasbin

That is correct. It only takes 400 billionaires to loot the United States of a massive $1.5 trillion. You've just won one million dollars!

The audience applauds. John Paulson yawns.

John Paulson

Who cares? I spend that much on silk ties each year.

The audience chuckles in amusement. Regis responds in kind.

Regis Hasbin

Very true, Mr. Paulson. Now, this next question is for a sizeable one hundred million dollars:

In 2010, was the percentage of the average billionaire's earnings paid in taxes...?

- A) Much higher than that paid by the average millionaire.
- B) Slightly higher than that paid by the average millionaire.
- C) The same as that paid by the average millionaire.
- D) Lower than that paid by the average millionaire.

John Paulson

I know this one. The answer is D, lower than that paid by the average millionaire.

Regis Hasbin

That is correct! As strange as it may seem, and despite all of the plutocrat's unceasing whining about excessive taxation, the unfathomably rich billionaire shelled out one of the lowest percentage tax returns in the history of the United States. Mr. Paulson, you've just won one hundred million dollars!

The crowd erupts into unrestrained applause. Paulson checks his Rolex watch for the time.

Regis Hasbin

Mr. Paulson, would you like to risk one hundred million dollars and try for our grand prize of one billion dollars?

John Paulson

Sure, but make it quick. I have to finish the last chapter of my new book, "The Courage to be Crooked".

Regis Hasbin

Sounds like an excellent read. Now, your question for one billion dollars is this:

When the world economy sank into a deep recession in 2009, did the fortunes of the world's billionaires as a whole...?

A) Fall sharply
B) Fall slightly
C) Stay the same
D) Rise dramatically

John Paulson

That's easy. Like for me, their fortunes rose dramatically despite the worldwide financial hardship that was being endured by the lowly masses. The answer is D.

Regis Hasbin

That is correct. The number of billionaires and their average net worth grew by leaps and bounds while the rest of the world suffered. You have just won $1 billion! What are you going to do now, Mr. Paulson?

John Paulson

I'm going to buy Disney World!

SOURCES

Round and Round We Go: *Forbes*, Oct.10, 2011

Forbes 400 Poor Farm: *Forbes*, Oct. 10, 2011

Citizen Gates: *Forbes,* Oct. 10, 2011

We're the Kings of the World: *Forbes*, Oct. 10, 2011 p., 39

Welcome to Buffettown: *Forbes*, Oct. 10, 2011, p. 210

Warren's in a New York State of Mind: *Forbes*, Oct. 10, 2011, p. 210

Take Me to Montego Bay: *Forbes*, Oct. 10, 2011, p. 214

One for the Money, 6,052 for the Show: *Forbes*, Oct. 10, 2011, p. 234

And Miles to Go Before He Sleeps: *Forbes*, Oct. 10, 2011, p. 214

The Kindergarten Billionaire Club: *Forbes*, Oct. 10, 2011, pp. 261,230,216

We Four Crooks: *Forbes,* Oct. 10, 2011, pp. 212, 214

All in the Family: *Forbes*, Oct. 10, 2011, pp. 262,268,270,274

It's Hard Out There for a Billionaire: "Workers Killed or Disabled on the Job" *Statistical Abstract of the United States: 2011*, p. 426, Table 656

Working in a Coal Mine: *Statistical Abstract of the United States: 2011*, p. 568, Table 895

You're Just Another Brick in the Wall: *Statistical Abstract of the United States: 2011*, p. 420, Table 646

It's Hard Out There for a Billionaire: *Forbes*, Oct. 10, 2011, p. 234

Look Ma, I've Got More Money Than a Bank!: *Statistical Abstract of the United States: 2011*, p. 737, Table 1178

The Forbes 400 Gang vs. the Largest Bank in the United States: *http://education.cardhub.com/bank-market-share-by-deposits/*

Come On, Take the Money and Run: *Forbes*, Oct. 10, 2011, p. 233

Welcome to Pottersville: *Statistical Abstract of the United States: 2011*, pp. 464,465

Oh, What a Pretty Pipe Dream It Is: *Forbes*, Oct. 10, 2011, p. 212 & *http://en.wikipedia.org/wiki/List_of_U.S._cities_by_population*

How Low Can You Go?: *Statistical Abstract of the United States: 2011*, p. 464

Blown Away by Those Billionaires: *http://en.wikipedia.org./wiki/Hurricane-Katrina*

Billionaires Just Want to Have Fun: *http://www.privilegeclub.com/tagldom-perignon-white-gold-jeroboam/*

Rich Man, Poor man: *Forbes,* Oct. 10, 2011, p.218

Keep Hope Alive: *Forbes*, Oct. 10, 2011, p. 242

Oprah Winfrey vs. the World: *The World Almanac and Book of Facts: 2011*, pp. 748, 760, 764, 770, 781, 782, 794, 798, 802, 803, 805,808, 827, 828, 831, 833, 841, 843, 848, 851

Michael Bloomberg vs. the World: *The World Almanac and Book of Facts: 2011*, pp. 751, 783, 784, 799,806, 818

Bill Gates vs. the World: *The World Almanac and Book of Facts: 2011*, pp. 754, 773, 791, 797, 800

The Forbes 400 Gang vs. the World: *The World Almanac and Book of Facts: 2011*, pp. 748, 749, 750, 753, 764, 768, 771, 780, 788, 832, 837

The Forbes 400 Military Superpower*:*
http://en.wikipedia.org/wiki/B-2_Spirt;
http://www.aerospaceweb.org/aircraft/bomber/f15 e/;
http://en.wikipedia.org/wiki/USS_George_H.W._Bush_(cvn-77) ;
http://en.wikipedia.org/Wiki/Virginia_class_submarine

A Really, Really, Really Big Bucket List*:*
http://news.travel.aol.com.2009/06/01/the-10-most-expensive-hotel-suites-in-the-world/

Back to Your Post, Slave: Statistical Abstract of the United States: 2011, p. 428

Fly Me to the Moon:
http://en.wikipedia.org/Wiki/United_States_one_dollar_bill ;
http://en.wikipedia.org/wiki/lunar_distance_(astronomy)

Up, Up, and Away:
*http://wiki.answers.com/Q/How_tall_is_1_Million
_dollars_in_100_dollar_bills*

The Forbes 400 Poor Farm: *Forbes*, Oct. 10,
2011, p. 261

Congratulation! The Greed Hall of Fame (John
Paulson): Forbes, Oct. 10, 2011, p. 216 &
*http://www.nytimes.com/2088/04/16/business/16W
all.html &
http://www.forbes.com/lists/2010/10/billionaires-
2010-John-Paulson_I69G.html*

I, Paulson:
*http://www.forbes.com/lists/2010/10/billionaires-
2010_John-Paulson_I69G.html*

Believe it or Not:
http://www.statista.com/statistics/220093/number-
of-billionaires-in-the-United-States/